CONTENTS

INTRODUCTION...

CLASSIC DAILY BREAD ....

    Julekake...

    Classic Dark Bread ....

    Craft Beer And Cheese Bread ....

    Bread Machine Bread 1

    Pumpernickel Bread..1

    Blue Cheese Bread 1

    Chocolate Coffee Bread...1

    Cheesy Sausage Loaf 1

    Cranberry Walnut Bread 1

    Lemon Blueberry Quick Bread 1

CHEESE & SWEET BREAD 1

    Jalapeno Cheddar Bread 1

    Jalapeño Corn Bread..2

    Buttermilk Pecan Bread 2

    Italian Cheese Bread 2

    Easy Donuts 2

    Chocolate Oatmeal Banana Bread...2

    Simple Cottage Cheese Bread 2

    Jalapeno Cheese Bread...2

    Spicy Cheese Bread..2

    Choco Chip Pumpkin Bread 2

BREAD FROM AROUND THE WORLD..2

    Sourdough 2

    Portuguese Corn Bread..3

Sweet Challa 32

Paleo Coconut Bread 33

Keto Pumpkin Bread 34

Italian Bread 35

German Pumpernickel Bread 36

Paleo And Dairy-free Bread 37

Low-carb Apple Bread 38

European Black Bread 39

SOURDOUGH BREAD 40

Basic Honey Bread 40

Multigrain Sourdough Bread 41

Herb Sourdough 42

Cheese Potato Bread 43

Classic White Bread 44

Basic Sourdough Bread 45

Pecan Cranberry Bread 46

Pecan Apple Spice Bread 47

Sourdough Milk Bread 48

Sourdough Cheddar Bread 49

FRUIT AND VEGETABLE BREAD 50

Cinnamon Apple Bread 50

Black Olive Bread 52

Curd Onion Bread With Sesame Seeds 53

Robust Date Bread 54

Banana Whole-wheat Bread 55

Gluten-free Best-ever Banana Bread 56

Tomato Herb Bread 57

Cinnamon Pumpkin Bread 58

Blueberry Honey Bread 60

Strawberry Shortcake Bread...6

SPICE, NUT & HERB BREAD 6

Fragrant Herb Bread...6

Raisin Seed Bread...6

Olive Bread...6

Chia Seed Bread...6

Pumpkin Coconut Almond Bread...6

Healthy Basil Whole Wheat Bread 6

Grain, Seed And Nut Bread...6

Simple Garlic Bread...6

Healthy Spelt Bread...7

Anise Lemon Bread...7

GLUTEN-FREE BREAD 7

Sandwich Bread...7

Gluten-free Whole Grain Bread...7

Paleo Bread...7

Cheese & Herb Bread...7

Gluten-free Oat & Honey Bread...7

Easy Gluten-free, Dairy-free Bread 7

Gluten-free Brown Bread...7

Italian Parmesan Cheese Bread 7

Gluten-free Pull-apart Rolls...8

Flax And Sunflower Seeds Bread...8

BASIC BREAD 8

Black Forest Loaf...8

Classic White Bread I...8

Golden Corn Bread...8

The Easiest Bread Maker Bread 8

Soft Sandwich Bread...8

Onion And Mushroom Bread 87

Vegan Cinnamon Raisin Bread 88

Whole Wheat Rolls 89

Vegan White Bread 90

Homemade Hot Dog And Hamburger Buns 91

PECIALTY BREAD 92

Holiday Eggnog Bread 92

Whole Grain Salt-free Bread 94

Coffee Caraway Seed Bread 95

Challah Bread 97

Cocoa Holiday Bread 99

Dry Fruit Cinnamon Bread 101

No-salt White Bread 103

New Year Spiced Bread 104

Low-carb Carrot Bread 106

Holiday Chocolate Bread...107

ECIPES INDEX 109

INTRODUCTION

As you know, bread making by hand is not a simple process. There are plenty of stirring, mixing, and kneading required. Stirring and kneading can be relatively painless for bread dough with lots of egg and butter to soften it up. But for tougher doughs, the manual labor involved could turn into a real chore. That's where a bread machine will really ease things up. A well built bread machine will automatically handle all the required dirty work, leaving you the creative work. Best of all, it does not take much other than the ability to push a few buttons to work a bread machine the way you want.

When considering a bread machine, it's a good idea to get familiar with its features and capabilities. Have an idea of how much you are looking to spend, these machines can run anywhere from below $60 to over $180, according to what brand, and what features you are looking for. Some have timers and delay buttons, while some don't, there is also the option of a crust setting which enables you to have light, medium, or dark crust on your bread loaf. You also need to know what type of breads you will be baking in your machine. If you're a big fan of making wheat bread, make sure that the bread machine your purchase has a cycle for it. Some bread machines have an extra special cycle for baking cakes and jams. Before deciding to purchase a bread machine, make sure that it has all the features you want and have enough cycles for all your baking needs. It' also a good idea to check for a cool down cycle, to prevent your bread loaf from becoming soggy, if you can't be there to remove it after the baking process is over. Most machines have a keep warm cycle to prevent sogginess, but some have a tendency to dry up the bread.

If a bread machine has multiple compartments, it could be a good idea, but it could also mean more maintenance and potential for mechanical problems. You can purchase bread machines that will produce different sizes and shapes of loaves, square, round and the traditional rectangle. Something else to look for in a bread machine is how easy it is to remove the bread ban for cleanup. To maintain your bread machine, it's good practice to check for the build up of crumbs. You do not have to do this often. I would suggest after every use, so as not to let the crumbs accumulate.

Like any appliance you plan to purchase for your kitchen, you should consider the size. You want to get a bread machine that is appropriate for your kitchen, not one that takes up all your extra counter space and be sure to check all the features and see if they fit your needs. Make sure your machine comes with a manual giving you instructions for operating your bread machine, because there are some models on the market that don't. You can choose to go for the cheaper model or the more expensive, the choice is up to you, but just remember, you get what you pay for.

CLASSIC DAILY BREAD

Julekake

Servings:14 Slices
Cooking Time: 3 H.

Ingredients:

- ⅓ cup evaporated milk
- ⅔ cup water
- 1 egg, room temperature
- 3⅓ cups bread flour
- ¼ cup sugar
- ½ tsp salt
- ½ tsp cardamom
- ½ cup softened butter, cut up
- 2¼ tsp dry active yeast
- ½ cup golden raisins
- ⅔ cup candied fruit

Directions:

1. Add each ingredient except the raisins to the bread machine in the order and at the temperature recommended by your bread machine manufacturer.
2. Close the lid, select the basic bread, low crust setting on your bread machine, and press start.
3. Add the raisins and fruit about 5 minutes before the kneading cycle has finished.
4. When the bread machine has finished baking, remove the bread and put it on a cooling rack.

Classic Dark Bread

Servings:1 Loaf
Cooking Time:x

Ingredients:

- 16 slice bread (2 pounds)
- 1¼ cups lukewarm water
- 2 tablespoons unsalted butter, melted
- ½ cup molasses
- ½ teaspoon table salt
- 1 cup rye flour
- 2½ cups white bread flour
- 2 tablespoons unsweetened cocoa powder
- Pinch ground nutmeg
- 2¼ teaspoons bread machine yeast
- 12 slice bread (1½ pounds)
- 1 cup lukewarm water
- 1½ tablespoons unsalted butter, melted
- ⅓ cup molasses
- ⅓ teaspoon table salt
- ¾ cup rye flour
- 2 cups white bread flour
- 1½ tablespoons unsweetened cocoa powder
- Pinch ground nutmeg
- 1⅔ teaspoons bread machine yeast

Directions:

1. Choose the size of loaf you would like to make and measure your ingredients.
2. Add the ingredients to the bread pan in the order listed above.
3. Place the pan in the bread machine and close the lid.
4. Turn on the bread maker. Select the White/Basic setting, then the loaf size, and finally the crust color. Start the cycle.
5. When the cycle is finished and the bread is baked, carefully remove the pan from the machine. Use a potholder as the handle will be very hot. Let rest for a few minutes.
6. Remove the bread from the pan and allow to cool on a wire rack for at least 10 minutes before slicing.

Nutrition:

- Info (Per Serving):Calories 143, fat 2.3 g, carbs 28.6 g, sodium 237 mg, protein 3.8 g

Craft Beer And Cheese Bread

Servings: 10

Cooking Time: 2 Hours 10 Minutes

Ingredients:

- 1 package active dry yeast
- 3 cups all-purpose flour
- 1 tablespoon sugar
- 1 1/2 teaspoons salt
- 1 tablespoon butter, room temperature
- 1 1/4 cups craft beer, at room temperature
- 1/2 cup cheddar cheese, shredded
- 1/2 cup Monterey Jack cheese, shredded

Directions:

1. Add beer to a sauce pan with cheese and heat on low until just warm; stir to blend.
2. Transfer mixture to the bread maker pan.
3. Measure and add dry ingredients (except yeast) to the bread pan. Make a small "hole" in the flour for the yeast.
4. Carefully pour the yeast into the "hole."
5. Snap the baking pan into the bread maker and close the lid.
6. Choose the Basic setting and preferred crust color and press Start.
7. When the loaf is done, remove the pan from the machine. After about 5 minutes, gently shake the pan to loosen the loaf and turn it out onto a rack to cool.
8. Serve warm.

Nutrition:

- Info Calories: 209, Sodium: 425 mg, Dietary Fiber: 1.2 g, Fat: 5.1 g, Carbs: 31.2 g, Protein: 7.1 g.

Bread Machine Bread

Servings:6
Cooking Time: 3 Hours And 25 Minutes

Ingredients:

- Flour – 2 cups, sifted
- Warm water – ¾ cup
- Sugar – 1 tsp.
- Active dry yeast – 1.25 tsp.
- Salt – 1 tsp.
- Oil – 1 tsp.

Directions:

1. Add ingredients according to bread machine recommendation.
2. Select the Basic setting and press Start.
3. Remove the loaf once it is baked.
4. Cool and slice.

Nutrition:

- Info (Per Serving): Calories: 163; Total Fat: 1 g; Saturated Fat: 0 g; Carbohydrates: 32 g; Cholesterol: 15 mg; Fiber: 1 g; Calcium: 18 mg; Sodium: 390 mg; Protein: 4 g

Pumpernickel Bread

Servings:1 Loaf

Cooking Time:x

Ingredients:

- 16 slice bread (2 pounds)
- 1 1/3 cups water, lukewarm between 80 and 90^{0}F
- 2 large eggs, room temperature and not cold
- ¼ cup oil
- ¼ cup honey
- 3 tablespoons dry milk powder
- ¼ cup cocoa powder
- 3 tablespoons caraway seeds
- 1 tablespoon instant coffee granules
- 2 teaspoons table salt
- 1 cup rye flour
- 1 cup whole wheat bread flour
- 2 cups white bread flour
- 2 ¼ teaspoons bread machine yeast
- 12 slice bread (1 ½ pounds)
- 3/4 cups water, lukewarm between 80 and 90^{0}F
- 2 large eggs, room temperature and not cold
- 2 tablespoons oil
- 2 tablespoons honey
- 3 tablespoons dry milk powder
- 3 tablespoons cocoa powder
- 2 tablespoons caraway seeds
- 2 teaspoon instant coffee granules
- 1 1/2 teaspoons table salt
- 3/4 cup rye flour
- 3/4 cup whole wheat bread flour
- 1 1/2 cups white bread flour
- 1 3/4 teaspoons bread machine yeast

Directions:

1. Choose the size of loaf you would like to make and measure your ingredients. If you want to make a 1-pound or 2 ½-pound loaf, please adjust your ingredient quantities accordingly. You can look at the conversion table at the end of the book for easy adjustments or click here.
2. Take the bread pan; add the ingredients in order listed above.
3. Secure the pan into the bread machine and close the lid.
4. Power the bread maker and select the option of the bread – White/Basic – then the size of the loaf you are making, and finally the crust color you desire. Start the machine.
5. After the bread cycle is done and the bread is cooked, carefully remove the pan from the machine. Use a potholder as the handle will be very hot. Let rest for a few minutes.
6. Remove the bread from the pan and allow to cool down on a wired rack for at least 10 minutes or more before slicing.

Nutrition:

- Info (Per Serving):Calories 134, fat 3.1 g, carbs 19 g, sodium 143 mg, protein 4.2 g

Blue Cheese Bread

Servings: 10 - 12
Cooking Time: 3 Hours

Ingredients:

- 3/4 cup warm water
- 1 large egg
- 1 teaspoon salt
- 3 cups bread flour
- 1 cup blue cheese, crumbled
- 2 tablespoons nonfat dry milk
- 2 tablespoons sugar
- 1 teaspoon bread machine yeast

Directions:

1. Add the ingredients to bread machine pan in the order listed above, (except yeast) ; be sure to add the cheese with the flour.
2. Make a well in the flour; pour the yeast into the hole.
3. Select Basic bread cycle, medium crust color, and press Start.
4. When finished, transfer to a cooling rack for 10 minutes and serve warm.

Nutrition:

- Info Calories: 171, Sodium: 266 mg, Dietary Fiber: 0.9 g, Fat: 3.9 g, Carbs: 26.8 g, Protein: 6.7 g.

Chocolate Coffee Bread

Servings:14 Slices
Cooking Time: 3 H.

Ingredients:

- 1⅓ cups water
- ⅓ cup cocoa powder
- 1⅓ cups bread flour
- 1⅓ cups whole wheat flour
- 3 Tbsp powdered milk
- ½ tsp salt
- 1½ Tbsp honey
- 2 envelopes instant mocha cappuccino mix
- 2¼ tsp active dry yeast
- ½ cup semi-sweet chocolate chips

Directions:

1. Add each ingredient except chips and mocha mix to the bread machine in the order and at the temperature recommended by your bread machine manufacturer.
2. Close the lid, select the sweet loaf, low crust setting on your bread machine, and press start.
3. Add the chocolate chips and mocha mix about 5 minutes before the kneading cycle has finished.
4. When the bread machine has finished baking, remove the bread and put it on a cooling rack.

Cheesy Sausage Loaf

Servings: 12
Cooking Time: 3 Hours

Ingredients:

- 1 cup warm water
- 4 teaspoons butter, softened
- 1 1/4 teaspoons salt
- 1 teaspoon sugar
- 3 cups bread flour
- 2 1/4 teaspoons active dry yeast
- 1 pound pork sausage roll, cooked and drained
- 1 1/2 cups Italian cheese, shredded
- 1/4 teaspoon garlic powder
- Pinch of black pepper
- 1 egg, lightly beaten
- Flour, for surface

Directions:

1. Add the first five ingredients to the bread maker pan in order listed above.
2. Make a well in the flour; pour the yeast into the hole.
3. Select Dough cycle and press Start.
4. Turn kneaded dough onto a lightly floured surface and roll into a 16-by-10-inch rectangle. Cover with plastic wrap and let rest for 10 minutes
5. Combine sausage, cheese, garlic powder and pepper in a mixing bowl.
6. Spread sausage mixture evenly over the dough to within one 1/2 inch of edges. Start with a long side and roll up like a jelly roll, pinch seams to seal, and tuck ends under.
7. Place the loaf seam-side down on a greased baking sheet. Cover and let rise in a warm place for 30 minutes.
8. Preheat an oven to 350°F and bake 20 minutes.
9. Brush with egg and bake an additional 15 to 20 minutes until golden brown.
10. Remove to a cooling rack and serve warm.

Nutrition:

- Info Calories: 172, Sodium: 350 mg, Dietary Fiber: 1.1 g, Fat: 4.7 g, Carbs: 27.1 g, Protein: 5.1 g.

Cranberry Walnut Bread

Servings:14 Slices
Cooking Time: 3 H.

Ingredients:

- ¼ cup water
- 1 egg
- 3 Tbsp honey
- 1½ tsp butter, softened
- 3¼ cups bread flour
- 1 cup milk
- 1 tsp salt
- ¼ tsp baking soda
- 1 tsp ground cinnamon
- 2½ tsp active dry yeast
- ¾ cup dried cranberries
- ½ cup chopped walnuts
- 1 Tbsp white vinegar
- ½ tsp sugar

Directions:

1. Add each ingredient except the berries and nuts to the bread machine in the order and at the temperature recommended by your bread machine manufacturer.
2. Close the lid, select the basic bread, medium crust setting on your bread machine, and press start.
3. Add the cranberries and walnuts around 5 minutes before the kneading cycle has finished
4. When the bread machine has finished baking, remove the bread and put it on a cooling rack.

Lemon Blueberry Quick Bread

Servings: 10 - 12
Cooking Time: 2 Hours

Ingredients:

- 2 cups all-purpose flour
- 1 1/2 teaspoons baking powder
- 1/2 teaspoon salt
- 1 tablespoon lemon zest
- 1 cup sugar
- 1/2 cup unsalted butter, softened
- 2 large eggs
- 2 teaspoons pure vanilla extract
- 1/2 cup whole milk
- 1 1/2 cups blueberries
- For the crumb topping:
- 1/3 cup sugar
- 3 tablespoons all-purpose flour
- 2 tablespoons butter, melted
- Non-stick cooking spray

Directions:

1. Spray bread maker pan with non-stick cooking spray and lightly flour.
2. Combine crumb topping ingredients and set aside.
3. In a small bowl, whisk together flour, baking powder and salt and set aside.
4. In a large mixing bowl, combine sugar and lemon zest. Add butter and beat until light and fluffy. Add eggs, vanilla and milk.
5. Add flour mixture and mix just until combine. Stir in blueberries and spread batter evenly into bread maker pan.
6. Top with crumb topping; select Sweet bread, light color crust, and press Start.
7. When done cool on a wire rack for 15 minutes and serve warm.

Nutrition:

- Info Calories: 462, Sodium: 332 mg, Dietary Fiber: 1 g, Fat: 32.1 g, Carbs: 41.8 g, Protein: 4 g.

CHEESE & SWEET BREAD

Jalapeno Cheddar Bread

Servings:1 Loaf
Cooking Time:x

Ingredients:
- 16 slice bread (2 pounds)
- 1⅓ cups lukewarm buttermilk
- ⅓ cup unsalted butter, melted
- 2 eggs, at room temperature
- ⅔ teaspoon table salt
- 1 jalapeno pepper, chopped
- ⅔ cup Cheddar cheese, shredded
- ⅓ cup sugar
- 2 cups all-purpose flour
- 1⅓ cups cornmeal
- 1½ tablespoons baking powder
- 12 slice bread (1½ pounds)
- 1 cup lukewarm buttermilk
- ¼ cup unsalted butter, melted
- 2 eggs, at room temperature
- ½ teaspoon table salt
- 1 jalapeno pepper, chopped
- ½ cup Cheddar cheese, shredded
- ¼ cup sugar
- 1⅓ cups all-purpose flour
- 1 cup cornmeal
- 1 tablespoon baking powder

Directions:

1. Choose the size of loaf you would like to make and measure your ingredients.
2. Add the ingredients to the bread pan in the order listed above.
3. Place the pan in the bread machine and close the lid.
4. Turn on the bread maker. Select the Rapid/Quick setting, then the loaf size, and finally the crust color. Start the cycle.
5. When the cycle is finished and the bread is baked, carefully remove the pan from the machine. Use a potholder as the handle will be very hot. Let rest for a few minutes.
6. Remove the bread from the pan and allow to cool on a wire rack for at least 10 minutes before slicing.

Nutrition:

- Info (Per Serving):Calories 173, fat 6.2 g, carbs 24.3 g, sodium 187 mg, protein 4.8 g

Jalapeño Corn Bread

Servings: 1 Loaf
Cooking Time: 10 Minutes

Ingredients:

- 12 to 16 slices bread (1½ to 2 pounds)
- 1 cup buttermilk, at 80°F to 90°F
- ¼ cup melted butter, cooled
- 2 eggs, at room temperature
- 1 jalapeño pepper, chopped
- 1⅓ cups all-purpose flour
- 1 cup cornmeal
- ½ cup (2 ounces) shredded Cheddar cheese
- ¼ cup sugar
- 1 tablespoon baking powder
- ½ teaspoon salt

Directions:

1. Preparing the Ingredients.
2. Choose the size of loaf of your preference and then measure the ingredients.
3. Add all of the ingredients mentioned previously in the list.
4. Close the lid after placing the pan in the bread machine.
5. Select the Bake cycle
6. Turn on the bread machine. Select the Quick/Rapid setting, select the loaf size, and the crust color. Press start.
7. When the cycle is finished, carefully remove the pan from the bread maker and let it rest.
8. Remove the bread from the pan, put in a wire rack to Cool about 5 minutes. Slice

Buttermilk Pecan Bread

Servings:1 Loaf

Cooking Time:x

Ingredients:

- 16 slice bread (2 pounds)
- 1 cup buttermilk, at room temperature
- 1 cup butter, at room temperature
- 1⅓ tablespoons instant coffee granules
- 3 eggs, at room temperature
- 1 cup sugar
- 3 cups all-purpose flour
- ⅔ tablespoon baking powder
- ⅔ teaspoon table salt
- 1⅓ cups chopped pecans
- 12 slice bread (1½ pounds)
- ¾ cup buttermilk, at room temperature
- ¾ cup butter, at room temperature
- 1 tablespoon instant coffee granules
- 3 eggs, at room temperature
- ¾ cup sugar
- 2 cups all-purpose flour
- ½ tablespoon baking powder
- ½ teaspoon table salt
- 1 cup chopped pecans

Directions:

1. Choose the size of loaf you would like to make and measure your ingredients.
2. Add the ingredients to the bread pan in the order listed above.
3. Place the pan in the bread machine and close the lid.
4. Turn on the bread maker. Select the Quick/Rapid setting, then the loaf size, and finally the crust color. Start the cycle.
5. When the cycle is finished and the bread is baked, carefully remove the pan from the machine. Use a potholder as the handle will be very hot. Let rest for a few minutes.
6. Remove the bread from the pan and allow to cool on a wire rack for at least 10 minutes before slicing.

Nutrition:

- Info (Per Serving):Calories 262, fat 14.3 g, carbs 26.4 g, sodium 217 mg, protein 4.7 g

Italian Cheese Bread

Servings: 14 Slices
Cooking Time: 10 Minutes

Ingredients:

- 1¼ cups water
- 3 cups bread flour
- ½ shredded pepper jack cheese
- 2 tsp Italian seasoning
- 2 Tbsp brown sugar
- 1½ tsp salt
- 2 tsp active dry yeast

Directions:

1. Preparing the Ingredients.
2. Add each ingredient to the bread machine in the order and at the temperature recommended by your bread machine manufacturer.
3. Select the Bake cycle
4. Close the lid, select the basic bread, medium crust setting on your bread machine, and press start.
5. When the bread machine has finished baking, remove the bread and put it on a cooling rack.

Easy Donuts

Servings: 12
Cooking Time: 1 Hour

Ingredients:

- 2/3 cups milk, room temperature
- 1/4 cup water, room temperature
- ½ cup of warm water
- 1/4 cup softened butter
- One egg slightly has beaten
- 1/4 cup granulated sugar
- 1 tsp salt
- 3 cups bread machine flour
- 2 1/2 tsp bread machine yeast
- oil for deep frying
- 1/4 cup confectioners' sugar

Directions:

1. Place the milk, water, butter, egg sugar, salt, flour, and yeast in a pan.
2. Select dough setting and push start. Press the start button.
3. When the process is complete, remove dough from the pan and transfer it to a lightly floured surface.
4. Using a rolling pin lightly dusted with flour, roll dough to ½ inch thickness.
5. Cut with a floured dusted donut cutter or circle cookie cutter.
6. Transfer donuts to a baking sheet that has been covered with wax paper. Place another layer of paper on top, then cover with a clean tea towel. Let rise 30-40 minutes.
7. Heat vegetable oil to 375º (190ºCº) in a deep-fryer or large, heavy pot.
8. Fry donuts 2-3 at a time until golden brown on both sides for about 3 minutes.
9. Drain on a paper towel.
10. Sprinkle with confectioners' sugar.

Nutrition:

- Info Calories 180;Carbohydrates: 30g;Total Fat 5g;Cholesterol 25mg;Protein 4g;Fiber 2g;Sugar 7g;Sodium 240mg;Potassium 64mg

Chocolate Oatmeal Banana Bread

Servings: 1 Loaf

Cooking Time: 10 Minutes Plus Fermenting Time

Ingredients:

- 12 to 16 slice bread (1½ to 2 pounds)
- 3 bananas, mashed
- 2 eggs, at room temperature
- ¾ cup packed light brown sugar
- ½ cup (1 stick) butter, at room temperature
- ½ cup sour cream, at room temperature
- ¼ cup sugar
- 1½ teaspoons pure vanilla extract
- 1 cup all-purpose flour
- ½ cup quick oats
- 2 tablespoons unsweetened cocoa powder
- 1 teaspoon baking soda

Directions:

1. Preparing the Ingredients.
2. Place the banana, eggs, brown sugar, butter, sour cream, sugar, and vanilla in your bread machine.
3. Program the machine for Quick/Rapid bread and press Start.
4. While the wet ingredients are mixing, stir together the flour, oats, cocoa powder, and baking soda in a small bowl.
5. Select the Bake cycle
6. After the first fast mixing is done and the machine signals, add the dry ingredients.
7. When the loaf is done, remove the bucket from the machine.
8. Let the loaf cool for 5 minutes.
9. Gently shake the bucket to remove the loaf, and turn it out onto a rack to cool.

Simple Cottage Cheese Bread

Servings: 1 Loaf
Cooking Time: 10 Minutes   Plus Fermenting Time

Ingredients:

- 12 slice bread (1½ pounds)
- ½ cup water, at 80°F to 90°F
- ¾ cup cottage cheese, at room temperature
- 1 egg, at room temperature
- 2 tablespoons butter, melted and cooled
- 1 tablespoon sugar
- 1 teaspoon salt
- ¼ teaspoon baking soda
- 3 cups white bread flour
- 2 teaspoons bread machine or instant yeast

Directions:

1. Preparing the Ingredients.
2. Choose the size of loaf of your preference and then measure the ingredients.
3. Add all of the ingredients mentioned previously in the list.
4. Close the lid after placing the pan in the bread machine.
5. Select the Bake cycle
6. Turn on the bread machine. Select the White/Basic setting, select the loaf size, and the crust color. Press start.
7. When the cycle is finished, carefully remove the pan from the bread maker and let it rest.
8. Remove the bread from the pan, put in a wire rack to Cool about 5 minutes. Slice

Jalapeno Cheese Bread

Servings:14 Slices
Cooking Time: 3 H.

Ingredients:

- 3 cups bread flour
- 1½ tsp active dry yeast
- 1 cup water
- 2 Tbsp sugar
- 1 tsp salt
- ½ cup shredded cheddar cheese
- ¼ cup diced jalapeno peppers

Directions:

1. Add each ingredient to the bread machine in the order and at the temperature recommended by your bread machine manufacturer.
2. Close the lid, select the basic bread, medium crust setting on your bread machine, and press start.
3. When the bread machine has finished baking, remove the bread and put it on a cooling rack.

Spicy Cheese Bread

Servings:15
Cooking Time: 3 Hours And 25 Minutes

Ingredients:

- Milk – 1 cup
- Unsalted butter – ½ cup, softened
- All-purpose flour – 3 cups
- Shredded cheddar cheese – 2 cups
- Garlic powder – ½ tsp.
- Salt – 2 tsp.
- Granulated sugar – 1 tbsp.
- Active dry yeast – ¼ oz.

Directions:

1. Add everything according to bread machine recommendations.
2. Select Basic cycle and Light crust.
3. Remove the bread when done.
4. Cool, slice, and serve.

Nutrition:

- Info (Per Serving): Calories: 16; Total Fat: 5.8 g; Saturated Fat: 3.6 g; Carbohydrates: 21 g; Cholesterol: 18 mg; Fiber: 0.7 g; Calcium: 132 mg; Sodium: 412 mg; Protein: 7 g

Choco Chip Pumpkin Bread

Servings: 10

Cooking Time: 2 Hours

Ingredients:

- Eggs – 2
- Chocolate chips – 1/3 cup.
- Brown sugar – 1 ½ cups.
- Vegetable oil – ½ cup.
- Can pumpkin puree – 15 oz.
- Baking powder – 1 tsp.
- Baking soda – 1 tsp.
- Cinnamon – 1 tsp.
- Pumpkin pie spice – 2 tsps.
- All-purpose flour – 2 cups.
- Salt – ½ tsp.

Directions:

1. Add all ingredients except for chocolate chips into the bread machine pan. Select quick bread setting then select light crust and press start. Add chocolate chips just before the final kneading cycle. Once loaf is done, remove the loaf pan from the machine. Allow it to cool for 10 minutes. Slice and serve.

BREAD FROM AROUND THE WORLD

Sourdough

Servings:1 Pound Loaf
Cooking Time: 3 Hours

Ingredients:

- for a sourdough starter:
- 2 cups white, all-purpose flour
- 1 tsp active dry yeast
- 2 cups lukewarm water
- for bread
- Sourdough starter :½ cup
- Lukewarm water :⅓ cup
- Sugar :½ tbsp
- Active dry yeast :½ tbsp
- Plain bread flour :1 ½ cups
- Vegetable oil :1 ½ tbsp
- Salt :1 tsp

Directions:

1. for a sourdough starter:
2. Combine the ingredients in a glass or ceramic dish. Ensure the dish is big enough to allow fo: expansion.
3. Cover the dish with cloth, fix the cloth into place using an elastic band.
4. Allow the starter to rest for five days in a warm area. Stir the starter once a day.
5. Your starter sourdough is now ready for use. Refrigerate the remainder and use it when needed. I you would like to make a few loaves, you can keep the sourdough starter "alive" by feeding it equa amounts of flour and water and allowing it to rest in a warm area and using it when needed.
6. for bread:
7. Add the sourdough starter, water, sugar, and yeast into the bread maker. Using a spatula, combine the ingredients.
8. Allow it to rest for ten minutes.
9. Add bread flour, oil, and salt.
10. Select the basic setting and medium crust function.
11. When ready, turn the bread out onto a drying rack and allow it to cool, then serve.

Nutrition:

- Info (Per Serving):Calories: 181.3 kcal / Total fat: 4.5 g / Saturated fat: 0.6 g Cholesterol: 0 mg Total carbohydrates: 30.4 g / Dietary fiber: 1.3 g / Sodium: 467 mg / Protein: 4.4 g

Portuguese Corn Bread

Servings: 8
Cooking Time: 2 Hours

Ingredients:

- 1 cup yellow cornmeal
- 1 1/4 cups cold water, divided
- 1 1/2 teaspoons active dry yeast
- 1 1/2 cups bread flour
- 2 teaspoons sugar
- 3/4 teaspoon salt
- 1 tablespoon olive oil

Directions:

1. Stir cornmeal into 3/4 cup of the cold water until lumps disappear.
2. Add cornmeal mixture and oil to bread maker pan.
3. Add remaining dry ingredients, except yeast, to pan.
4. Make a well in the center of the dry ingredients and add the yeast.
5. Choose Sweet bread cycle, light crust color and press Start.
6. Transfer to plate and serve warm.

Nutrition:

- Info Calories: 108, Sodium: 152 mg, Dietary Fiber: 1.3 g, Fat: 1.7 g, Carbs: 20.6 g, Protein: 2.6 g

Sweet Challa

Servings: 1 Loaf
Cooking Time: 45 Minutes

Ingredients:

- 1 ½ cup cream cheese
- 1 cup protein powder, unflavored and unsweetened
- 2/3 cup protein powder, vanilla flavour and unsweetened
- 1/3 cup no-calorie sweetener of your choice
- ¼ cup dried cranberries
- ¼ cup butter
- ¼ cup almond flour
- 2 ½ teaspoons baking powder
- One teaspoon xanthan gum
- ½ teaspoon salt
- 1/3 teaspoon salt
- Four eggs, beaten
- ¼ cup heavy cream
- ¼ cup oil

Directions:

1. Set aside two tablespoons of the beaten eggs for later use.
2. Put the wet ingredients first, then the dry ingredients into the bread pan.
3. Press the "Manual" or "Dough" setting on the bread machine.
4. Once completed, transfer the dough to a surface that has been lightly dusted with almond flour.
5. Remove the air bubbles by punching the dough.
6. Divide the dough into 3.
7. Roll each piece until it becomes 16 inches long.
8. Braid the three pieces together on a lightly greased baking sheet.
9. Allow the dough to rise for about 30 minutes while preheating the oven to 4000F.
10. Brush the dough on the top with the reserved eggs from earlier.
11. Bake for 45 minutes, or until it is golden brown.

Nutrition:

- Info Calories: 158;Carbohydrates: 2g;Fat: 13g;Protein: 9g

Paleo Coconut Bread

Servings: 10 Pcs
Cooking Time: 50 Minutes

Ingredients:
- ½ cup coconut flour
- ¼ cup almond milk (unsweetened)
- ¼ cup coconut oil (melted)
- 6 eggs
- ¼ tsp. baking soda
- ¼ tsp. salt

Directions:
1. Preheat the oven to 350F.
2. Prepare a (8 x 4) bread pan with parchment paper.
3. In a bowl, combine salt, baking soda, and coconut flour.
4. Combine the oil, milk, and eggs in another bowl.
5. Gradually add the wet ingredients into the dry ingredients and mix well.
6. Pour the mixture into the prepared pan.
7. Bake for 40 to 50 minutes.
8. Cool, slice, and serve.

Nutrition:
- Info Calories: 108;Fat: 8.7g;Carb: 3.4g;Protein: 4.2g

Keto Pumpkin Bread

Servings: 1 Loaf

Cooking Time: 1 Hour And 30 Minutes

Ingredients:

- 1 ½ cup almond flour
- ½ cup coconut flour
- 2/3 cup no-calorie sweetener of your choice
- ½ cup butter softened
- One teaspoon cinnamon
- ½ teaspoon nutmeg
- ½ teaspoon salt
- ¼ teaspoon ginger, grated
- 1/8 teaspoon ground cloves
- Four eggs
- ¾ cup pumpkin puree
- Four teaspoons baking powder
- One teaspoon vanilla extract

Directions:

1. Add the wet ingredients followed by dry ingredients into the bread pan.
2. Use the "Quick" or "Cake" mode of the bread machine.
3. Wait until the cycles are done.
4. Remove the pan from the machine, but take out the bread from the pan for 10 mins.
5. Let the bread cool down first before slicing it completely.

Nutrition:

- Info Calories: 242;Carbohydrates: 11g;Fat: 20g;Protein: 7g

Italian Bread

Servings: 2 Loaves
Cooking Time: 1 Hour And 10 Minutes

Ingredients:

- One tablespoon of light brown sugar
- 4 cups all-purpose flour, unbleached
- 1 ½ teaspoon of salt
- One 1/3 cups + 1 tablespoon warm water
- One package active dry yeast
- 1 ½ teaspoon of olive oil
- One egg
- Two tablespoons cornmeal

Directions:

1. Place flour, brown sugar, 1/3 cup warm water, salt, olive oil, and yeast in your bread machine. Select the dough cycle. Hit the start button.
2. Deflate your dough. Turn it on a floured surface.
3. Form two loaves from the dough.
4. Keep them on your cutting board. The seam side should be down. Sprinkle some cornmeal on your board.
5. Place a damp cloth on your loaves to cover them.
6. Wait for 40 minutes. The volume should double.
7. In the meantime, preheat your oven to 190 °C.
8. Beat 1 tablespoon of water and an egg in a bowl.
9. Brush this mixture on your loaves.
10. Make an extended cut at the center of your loaves with a knife.
11. Shake your cutting board gently, making sure that the loaves do not stick.
12. Now slide your loaves on a baking sheet.
13. Bake in your oven for about 35 minutes.

Nutrition:

- Info Calories 105;Carbohydrates: 20.6 g;Total Fat 0.9 g;Cholesterol 9 mg;Protein 3.1 g;Fiber 1 g;Sugar 1g;Sodium 179 mg;Potassium 39 mg

German Pumpernickel Bread

Servings: 1 Loaf

Cooking Time: 1 Hour And 10 Minutes

Ingredients:

- 1 1/2 tablespoon vegetable oil
- 1 1/8 cups warm water
- Three tablespoons cocoa
- 1/3 cup molasses
- 1 ½ teaspoons salt
- One tablespoon caraway seeds
- 1 cup rye flour
- 1 ½ cups of bread flour
- 1 ½ tablespoon wheat gluten
- 1 cup whole wheat flour
- 2 ½ teaspoons bread machine yeast

Directions:

1. Put everything in your bread machine.
2. Select the primary cycle.
3. Hit the start button.
4. Transfer bread to a rack for cooling once done.

Nutrition:

- Info Calories 119;Carbohydrates: 22.4 g;Total Fat 2.3 g;Cholesterol 0mg;Protein 3 g;Sodium 295 mg

Paleo And Dairy-free Bread

Servings:1 Pound Loaf
Cooking Time: 3 Hours

Ingredients:

- Flax meal :¼ cup
- Chia seeds :2 tbsp
- Coconut oil, melted :⅛ cup
- Egg :1 ½
- Almond milk :¼ cup
- Honey :½ tbsp
- Almond flour :1 cup
- Tapioca flour :⅔ cup
- Coconut flour :⅛ cup
- Salt :½ tsp
- Cream of tartar :1 tsp
- Bread machine yeast :1 tsp

Directions:

1. In a mixing bowl, combine one tablespoon of flax meal with the chia seeds. Stir in the water and set aside.
2. In a separate mixing bowl, pour in the melted coconut oil, eggs, almond milk, and honey. Whisk together. Followed by whisking in the flax meal and chia seed mixture. Pour this into the bread machine.
3. In a mixing bowl, combine the almond, tapioca, and coconut flour. Add the remainder of the flax meal and salt. Add in the cream of tartar and baking soda.
4. Pour the dry ingredients on top of the wet ingredients.
5. Finish by adding the yeast.
6. Select the whole wheat setting and medium crust function.
7. When ready, turn the bread out onto a drying rack and allow it to cool, then serve.

Nutrition:

- Info (Per Serving):Calories: 142 kcal / Total fat: 6.3 g / Saturated fat: 1.8g / Cholesterol: 34.9 mg / Total carbohydrates: 15.5 g / Dietary fiber: 4.4 g / Sodium: 236.8 mg / Protein: 4.1 g

Low-carb Apple Bread

Servings: 1 Loaf

Cooking Time: 1 Hour And 30 Minutes

Ingredients:

- Two apples, peeled and chopped
- 2 cups almond flour
- ½ cup golden flaxseed, milled
- ½ cup no-calorie sweetener of your choice
- Two teaspoons cinnamon
- ¾ teaspoon baking soda
- ¾ teaspoon salt
- ½ teaspoon nutmeg
- Four eggs, lightly beaten
- ¼ cup of water
- ¼ cup heavy cream
- Four tablespoons coconut oil
- Two teaspoons vanilla extract
- 1 ½ teaspoon apple cider vinegar

Directions:

1. Place all ingredients in the pan according to the order specified above.
2. Set the bread machine to "Cake" or "Quick" mode.
3. Let the cycles finish.
4. Remove the bread pan from the machine, but keep the bread in the pan for another 10 minutes.
5. Slice the bread only when it has cooled down.

Nutrition:

- Info Calories: 242;Carbohydrates: 11g;Fat: 20g;Protein: 7g

European Black Bread

Servings: 1 Loaf

Cooking Time: 1 Hour And 5 Minutes

Ingredients:

- ¾ teaspoon cider vinegar
- 1 cup of water
- ½ cup rye flour
- 1 ½ cups flour
- One tablespoon margarine
- ¼ cup of oat bran
- One teaspoon salt
- 1 ½ tablespoons sugar
- One teaspoon dried onion flakes
- One teaspoon caraway seed
- One teaspoon yeast
- Two tablespoons unsweetened cocoa

Directions:

1. Put everything in your bread machine.
2. Now select the basic setting.
3. Hit the start button.
4. Transfer bread to a rack for cooling once done.

Nutrition:

- Info Calories 114;Carbohydrates: 22 g;Total Fat 1.7 g;Cholesterol 0mg;Protein 3 g;Sugar 2 g;Sodium 247 mg

SOURDOUGH BREAD

Basic Honey Bread

Servings: 1 Loaf
Cooking Time: 10 Minutes

Ingredients:

- 12 slice bread (1½ pounds)
- 1½ cups warm milk
- ¼ cup unsalted butter, melted
- 2 eggs, beaten
- 1 teaspoon apple cider vinegar
- ½ cup honey
- 1 teaspoon table salt
- 3 cups gluten-free flour(s) of your choice
- 1½ teaspoons xanthan gum
- 1¾ teaspoons bread machine yeast

Directions:

1. Preparing the Ingredients.
2. Choose the size of loaf of your preference and then measure the ingredients.
3. Add all of the ingredients mentioned previously in the list, close the lid after placing the pan in the bread machine.
4. Select the Bake cycle
5. Turn on the bread machine. Select the White/Basic or Gluten-Free (if your machine has this setting) setting, select the loaf size, and the crust color. Press start.
6. When the cycle is finished, carefully remove the pan from the bread maker and let it rest.
7. Remove the bread from the pan, put in a wire rack to cool for at least 10 minutes, and slice.

Multigrain Sourdough Bread

Servings: 1 Loaf

Cooking Time: 10 Minutes

Ingredients:

- 12 slice bread (1½ pounds)
- ⅔ cup water, at 80°F to 90°F
- ¾ cup Simple Sourdough Starter, fed, active, and at room temperature
- 2 tablespoons melted butter, cooled
- 2½ tablespoons sugar
- ¾ teaspoon salt
- ¾ cup multigrain cereal
- 2⅔ cups white bread flour
- 1½ teaspoons bread machine or instant yeast

Directions:

1. Preparing the Ingredients.
2. Choose the size of loaf of your preference and then measure the ingredients.
3. Add all of the ingredients mentioned previously in the list, close the lid after placing the pan in the bread machine.
4. Select the Bake cycle
5. Turn on the bread machine. Select the Wheat/Whole-Grain bread setting, select the loaf size, and the crust color. Press start. When the cycle is finished, carefully remove the pan from the bread maker and let it rest.
6. Remove the bread from the pan, put in a wire rack to cool for at least 10 minutes, and slice.

Herb Sourdough

Servings: 1 Loaf
Cooking Time: 10 Minutes

Ingredients:
- 8 slice bread (1 pound)
- 1⅓ cups No-Yeast Sourdough Starter, fed, active, and at room temperature
- 4 teaspoons water, at 80°F to 90°F
- 4 teaspoons melted butter, cooled
- 1⅓ teaspoons sugar
- 1 teaspoon salt
- 1 teaspoon chopped fresh basil
- 1 teaspoon chopped fresh oregano
- ½ teaspoon chopped fresh thyme
- 1⅔ cups white bread flour
- 1 teaspoon bread machine or instant yeast

Directions:
1. Preparing the Ingredients.
2. Choose the size of loaf of your preference and then measure the ingredients.
3. Add all of the ingredients mentioned previously in the list, close the lid after placing the pan in the bread machine
4. Select the Bake cycle
5. Turn on the bread machine. Select the Wheat/Whole-Grain bread setting, select the loaf size, and the crust color. Press start. When the cycle is finished, carefully remove the pan from the bread maker and let it rest.
6. Remove the bread from the pan, put in a wire rack to cool for at least 5 minutes, and slice

Cheese Potato Bread

Servings: 1 Loaf
Cooking Time: 10 Minutes

Ingredients:

- 12 slice bread (1½ pounds)
- 1 cup lukewarm water
- 2¼ tablespoons vegetable oil
- 2 large eggs, beaten
- ⅓ cup dry skim milk powder
- 3 tablespoons sugar
- ¾ teaspoon apple cider vinegar
- 1⅛ teaspoons table salt
- ⅓ cup cornstarch
- ½ cup cottage cheese
- 3 tablespoons snipped chives
- ⅓ cup instant potato buds
- ⅓ cup potato starch
- ⅓ cup tapioca flour
- 1½ cups white rice flour
- 1½ teaspoons bread machine yeast

Directions:

1. Preparing the Ingredients.
2. Choose the size of loaf of your preference and then measure the ingredients.
3. Add all of the ingredients mentioned previously in the list, close the lid after placing the pan in the bread machine.
4. Select the Bake cycle
5. Turn on the bread machine. Select the White/ Basic or Gluten-Free (if your machine has this setting) setting, select the loaf size, and the crust color. Press start.
6. When the cycle is finished, carefully remove the pan from the bread maker and let it rest.
7. Remove the bread from the pan, put in a wire rack to cool for at least 10 minutes, and slice.

Classic White Bread

Servings: 1 Loaf
Cooking Time: 10 Minutes

Ingredients:
- 12 slice bread (1½ pounds)
- 1¼ cup lukewarm water
- 3 tablespoons canola oil
- ¾ teaspoon apple cider vinegar
- 2 eggs, room temperature, slightly beaten
- 1½ cups white rice flour
- ⅔ cup tapioca flour
- ½ cup nonfat dry milk powder
- ½ cup potato starch
- ⅓ cup cornstarch
- 2 tablespoon sugar
- ⅔ tablespoon xanthan gum
- ⅔ teaspoon table salt
- 1¼ teaspoons bread machine yeast

Directions:
1. Preparing the Ingredients.
2. Choose the size of loaf of your preference and then measure the ingredients.
3. Add all of the ingredients mentioned previously in the list, close the lid after placing the pan in the bread machine.
4. Select the Bake cycle
5. Turn on the bread machine. Select the White/Basic setting, select the loaf size, and the crust color. Press start.
6. When the cycle is finished, carefully remove the pan from the bread maker and let it rest.
7. Remove the bread from the pan, put in a wire rack to cool for at least 10 minutes, and slice.

Basic Sourdough Bread

Servings: 1 Loaf
Cooking Time: 10 Minutes

Ingredients:

- 12 slice bread (1½ pounds)
- 2 cups Simple Sourdough Starter (here), fed, active, and at room temperature
- 2 tablespoons water, at 80°F to 90°F
- ¾ teaspoon apple cider vinegar
- 1⅓ teaspoons sugar
- 1 teaspoon salt
- 1⅔ cups white bread flour
- ½ cup nonfat dry milk powder
- 1 teaspoon bread machine or instant yeast

Directions:

1. Preparing the Ingredients.
2. Choose the size of loaf of your preference and then measure the ingredients.
3. Add all of the ingredients mentioned previously in the list, close the lid after placing the pan in the bread machine.
4. Select the Bake cycle
5. Turn on the bread machine. Select the White/Basic setting, select the loaf size, and the crust color. Press start.
6. When the cycle is finished, carefully remove the pan from the bread maker and let rest. When the machine signals to add ingredients, add the chopped pecans.
7. Remove the bread from the pan, put in a wire rack to cool for at least 5 minutes, and slice.

Pecan Cranberry Bread

Servings: 1 Loaf
Cooking Time: 10 Minutes

Ingredients:
- 12 slice bread (1½ pounds)
- 1⅛ cups lukewarm water
- 3 tablespoons canola oil
- ¾ tablespoon orange zest
- ¾ teaspoon apple cider vinegar
- 2 eggs, slightly beaten
- 2¼ tablespoons sugar
- ¾ teaspoon table salt
- 1½ cups white rice flour
- ½ cup nonfat dry milk powder
- ⅓ cup tapioca flour
- ⅓ cup potato starch
- ¼ cup corn starch
- ¾ tablespoon xanthan gum
- 1½ teaspoons bread machine yeast
- ½ cup dried cranberries
- ½ cup pecan pieces

Directions:
1. Preparing the Ingredients.
2. Choose the size of loaf of your preference and then measure the ingredients.
3. Add all of the ingredients mentioned previously in the list, close the lid after placing the pan in the bread machine. Select the Bake cycle
4. Turn on the bread maker. Select the Gluten Free or Fruit/Nut (if your machine has this setting) setting, then the loaf size, and finally the crust color. Start the cycle. (If you don't have either of the above settings, use Basic/White.).
5. When the machine signals to add ingredients, add the pecans and cranberries. (Some machines have a fruit/nut hopper where you can add the pecans and cranberries when you start the machine. The machine will automatically add them to the dough during the baking process.).
6. When the cycle is finished, carefully remove the pan from the bread maker and let it rest.
7. Remove the bread from the pan, put in a wire rack to cool for at least 10 minutes, and slice.

Pecan Apple Spice Bread

Servings: 1 Loaf
Cooking Time: 10 Minutes

Ingredients:

- 12 slice bread (1½ pounds)
- ⅓ cup lukewarm water
- 2¼ tablespoons canola oil
- ¾ teaspoon apple cider vinegar
- 2¼ tablespoons light brown sugar, packed
- ¾ cup Granny Smith apples, grated
- 2 eggs, room temperature, slightly beaten
- ½ cup nonfat dry milk powder
- ½ cup brown rice flour
- ½ cup tapioca flour
- ½ cup millet flour
- ⅓ cup corn starch
- 1½ tablespoons apple pie spice
- ¾ tablespoon xanthan gum
- ¾ teaspoon table salt
- 1¼ teaspoons bread machine yeast
- ⅓ cup pecans, chopped

Directions:

1. Preparing the Ingredients.
2. Choose the size of loaf of your preference and then measure the ingredients.
3. Add all of the ingredients mentioned previously in the list, close the lid after placing the pan in the bread machine.
4. Select the Bake cycle
5. Turn on the bread machine. Select the White/Basic setting, select the loaf size, and the crust color. Press start.
6. When the cycle is finished, carefully remove the pan from the bread maker and let rest. When the machine signals to add ingredients, add the chopped pecans.
7. Remove the bread from the pan, put in a wire rack to cool for at least 10 minutes, and slice.

Sourdough Milk Bread

Servings: 1 Loaf
Cooking Time: 10 Minutes

Ingredients:

- 12 slice bread (1½ pounds)
- 1½ cups Simple Sourdough Starter (here) or No-Yeast Sourdough Starter (here), fed, active, and a
  room temperature
- ⅓ cup milk, at 80°F to 90°F
- 3 tablespoons olive oil
- 1½ tablespoons honey
- 1 teaspoon salt
- 3 cups white bread flour
- 1 teaspoon bread machine or instant yeast

Directions:

1. Preparing the Ingredients.
2. Choose the size of loaf of your preference and then measure the ingredients.
3. Add all of the ingredients mentioned previously in the list, close the lid after placing the pan in the
   bread machine.
4. Select the Bake cycle
5. Turn on the bread machine. Select the White/Basic setting, select the loaf size, and the crust color
   Press start.
6. When the cycle is finished, carefully remove the pan from the bread maker and let it rest.
7. Remove the bread from the pan, put in a wire rack to cool for at least 10 minutes, and slice.

Sourdough Cheddar Bread

Servings: 1 Loaf
Cooking Time: 10 Minutes

Ingredients:

- 12 slice bread (1½ pounds)
- 1 cup Simple Sourdough Starter or No-Yeast Sourdough Starter, fed, active, and at room temperature
- ⅓ cup water, at 80°F to 90°F
- 4 teaspoons sugar
- 1 teaspoon salt
- ½ cup (2 ounces) grated aged Cheddar cheese
- ⅔ cup whole-wheat flour
- ¼ cup oat bran
- 1⅓ cups white bread flour
- 1½ teaspoons bread machine or instant yeast

Directions:

1. Preparing the Ingredients.
2. Choose the size of loaf of your preference and then measure the ingredients.
3. Add all of the ingredients mentioned previously in the list, close the lid after placing the pan in the bread machine
4. Select the Bake cycle
5. Turn on the bread machine. Select the Wheat/Whole-Grain bread setting, select the loaf size, and the crust color. Press start. When the cycle is finished, carefully remove the pan from the bread maker and let it rest.
6. Remove the bread from the pan, put in a wire rack to cool for at least 5 minutes, and slice.

FRUIT AND VEGETABLE BREAD

Cinnamon Apple Bread

Servings:1 Loaf
Cooking Time:x

Ingredients:
- 16 slice bread (2 pounds)
- 1⅓ cups lukewarm milk
- 3⅓ tablespoons butter, melted
- 2⅔ tablespoons sugar
- 2 teaspoons table salt
- 1⅓ teaspoons cinnamon, ground
- A pinch ground cloves
- 4 cups white bread flour
- 2¼ teaspoons bread machine yeast
- 1⅓ cups peeled apple, finely diced
- 12 slice bread (1½ pounds)
- 1 cup lukewarm milk
- 2½ tablespoons butter, melted
- 2 tablespoons sugar
- 1½ teaspoons table salt
- 1 teaspoon cinnamon, ground
- Pinch ground cloves
- 3 cups white bread flour
- 2¼ teaspoons bread machine yeast
- 1 cup peeled apple, finely diced

Directions:

1. Choose the size of loaf you would like to make and measure your ingredients.
2. Add all of the ingredients except for the apples to the bread pan in the order listed above.
3. Place the pan in the bread machine and close the lid.
4. Turn on the bread maker. Select the White/Basic or Fruit/Nut (if your machine has this setting) setting, then the loaf size, and finally the crust color. Start the cycle.
5. When the machine signals to add ingredients, add the apples. (Some machines have a fruit/nut hopper where you can add the apples when you start the machine. The machine will automatically add them to the dough during the baking process.)
6. When the cycle is finished and the bread is baked, carefully remove the pan from the machine. Use a potholder as the handle will be very hot. Let rest for a few minutes.
7. Remove the bread from the pan and allow to cool on a wire rack for at least 10 minutes before slicing.

Nutrition:

- Info (Per Serving):Calories 174, fat 2.3 g, carbs 26.4 g, sodium 286 mg, protein 4.6 g

Black Olive Bread

Servings: 1 Loaf
Cooking Time: 10 Minutes

Ingredients:

- 12 slices (1½ pounds)
- 1 cup milk, at 80°F to 90°F
- 1½ tablespoons melted butter, cooled
- 1 teaspoon minced garlic
- 1½ tablespoons sugar
- 1 teaspoon salt
- 3 cups white bread flour
- 1 teaspoon bread machine or instant yeast
- ⅓ cup chopped black olives

Directions:

1. Preparing the Ingredients.
2. Choose the size of loaf of your preference and then measure the ingredients.
3. Add all of the ingredients mentioned previously in the list. Close the lid after placing the pan in the bread machine.
4. Select the Bake cycle
5. Turn on the bread machine. Select the White/Basic setting, select the loaf size, and the crust color Press start.
6. When the cycle is finished, carefully remove the pan from the bread maker and let it rest.
7. Remove the bread from the pan, put in a wire rack to cool for at least 10 minutes.

Curd Onion Bread With Sesame Seeds

Servings: 8 Pcs

Cooking Time: 1 Hour And 30 Minutes

Ingredients:

- ¾ cup of water
- 3 2/3 cups wheat flour
- ¾ cup cottage cheese
- Two tablespoons softened butter
- Two tablespoon sugar
- 1 ½ teaspoons salt
- 1 ½ tablespoon sesame seeds
- Two tablespoons dried onions
- One ¼ teaspoons dry yeast

Directions:

1. Put the products in the bread maker according to its instructions.
2. Bake on the BASIC program.

Nutrition:

- Info Calories 277;Total Fat 4.7g;Saturated Fat 2.3g;Cholesterol 9g;Sodium 547mg;Total Carbohydrate 48.4g;Dietary Fiber 1.9g;Total Sugars 3.3g;Protein 9.4g

Robust Date Bread

Servings: 1 Loaf
Cooking Time: 10 Minutes

Ingredients:
- 12 slice bread (1½ pounds)
- ¾ cup water, at 80°F to 90°F
- ½ cup milk, at 80°F
- 2 tablespoons melted butter, cooled
- ¼ cup honey
- 3 tablespoons molasses
- 1 tablespoon sugar
- 2 tablespoons skim milk powder
- 1 teaspoon salt
- 2¼ cups whole-wheat flour
- 1¼ cups white bread flour
- 1 tablespoon unsweetened cocoa powder
- 1½ teaspoons bread machine or instant yeast
- ¾ cup chopped dates

Directions:
1. Preparing the Ingredients.
2. Choose the size of loaf of your preference and then measure the ingredients.
3. Add all of the ingredients mentioned previously in the list. Close the lid after placing the pan in the bread machine
4. Select the Bake cycle
5. Turn on the bread machine. Select the White/Basic setting, select the loaf size, and the crust color. Press start.
6. When the cycle is finished, carefully remove the pan from the bread maker and let it rest.
7. Remove the bread from the pan, put in a wire rack to cool for at least 10 minutes before slicing.

Banana Whole-wheat Bread

Servings: 1 Loaf
Cooking Time: 10 Minutes

Ingredients:

- 12 slice bread (1½ pounds)
- ½ cup milk, at 80°F to 90°F
- 1 cup mashed banana
- 1 egg, at room temperature
- 1½ tablespoons melted butter, cooled
- 3 tablespoons honey
- 1 teaspoon pure vanilla extract
- ½ teaspoon salt
- 1 cup whole-wheat flour
- 1¼ cups white bread flour
- 1½ teaspoons bread machine or instant yeast

Directions:

1. Preparing the Ingredients.
2. Choose the size of loaf of your preference and then measure the ingredients.
3. Add all of the ingredients mentioned previously in the list. Close the lid after placing the pan in the bread machine
4. Select the Bake cycle.
5. Turn on the bread machine. Select the Sweet bread setting, select the loaf size, and the crust color. Press start. When the cycle is finished, carefully remove the pan from the bread maker and let it rest.
6. Shake the bucket to remove the loaf, and turn it out onto a rack to cool.

Gluten-free Best-ever Banana Bread

Servings: 1 Loaf
Cooking Time: 10 Minutes

Ingredients:

- 16 slices bread
- ½ cup tapioca flour
- ½ cup white rice flour
- ½ cup potato starch
- ¼ cup garbanzo and fava flour
- ¼ cup sweet white sorghum flour
- 1 teaspoon xanthan gum
- ½ teaspoon guar gum
- 1 teaspoon gluten-free baking powder
- 1 teaspoon baking soda
- 1 teaspoon salt
- 1 teaspoon ground cinnamon
- ¾ cup packed brown sugar
- 1 cup mashed very ripe bananas (2 medium)
- ½ cup ghee (measured melted)
- ¼ cup almond milk, soymilk or regular milk
- 1 teaspoon gluten-free vanilla
- 2 eggs

Directions:

1. Preparing the Ingredients.
2. Choose the size of loaf of your preference and then measure the ingredients. Add all of the ingredients mentioned previously in the list. Close the lid after placing the pan in the bread machine.
3. Select the Bake cycle
4. Turn on the bread machine. Select the White/Basic setting, select the loaf size, and the crust color. Press start.
5. When the cycle is finished, carefully remove the pan from the bread maker and let it rest. Remove the bread from the pan, put in a wire rack to Cool about 1 hour.

Tomato Herb Bread

Servings: 1 Loaf
Cooking Time: 10 Minutes

Ingredients:

- 8 slice bread (1 pounds)
- ½ cup tomato sauce, at 80°F to 90°F
- ½ tablespoon olive oil
- ½ tablespoon sugar
- 1 tablespoon dried basil
- ½ tablespoon dried oregano
- ½ teaspoon salt
- 2 tablespoons grated Parmesan cheese
- 1½ cups white bread flour
- 1⅛ teaspoons bread machine or instant yeast

Directions:

1. Preparing the Ingredients.
2. Choose the size of loaf of your preference and then measure the ingredients.
3. Add all of the ingredients mentioned previously in the list.
4. Close the lid after placing the pan in the bread machine.
5. Select the Bake cycle
6. Turn on the bread machine. Select the White/Basic setting, select the loaf size, and the crust color. Press start.
7. When the cycle is finished, carefully remove the pan from the bread maker and let it rest.
8. Remove the bread from the pan, put in a wire rack to Cool about 5 minutes. Slice

Cinnamon Pumpkin Bread

Servings:1 Loaf
Cooking Time:x

Ingredients:

- 16 slice bread (2 pounds)
- 2 cups pumpkin puree
- 4 eggs, slightly beaten
- ½ cup unsalted butter, melted
- 1¼ cups sugar
- ½ teaspoon table salt
- 4 cups white bread flour
- 1 teaspoon cinnamon, ground
- ¾ teaspoon baking soda
- ½ teaspoon nutmeg, ground
- ½ teaspoon ginger, ground
- Pinch ground cloves
- 2 teaspoons baking powder
- 12 slice bread (1½ pounds)
- 1½ cups pumpkin puree
- 3 eggs, slightly beaten
- ⅓ cup unsalted butter, melted
- 1 cup sugar
- ¼ teaspoon table salt
- 3 cups white bread flour
- ¾ teaspoon cinnamon, ground
- ½ teaspoon baking soda
- ¼ teaspoon nutmeg, ground
- ¼ teaspoon ginger, ground
- Pinch ground cloves
- 1½ teaspoons baking powder

Directions:

1. Choose the size of loaf you would like to make and measure your ingredients.
2. Add the ingredients to the bread pan in the order listed above.
3. Place the pan in the bread machine and close the lid.
4. Turn on the bread maker. Select the Quick/Rapid setting, then the loaf size, and finally the crust color. Start the cycle.
5. When the cycle is finished and the bread is baked, carefully remove the pan from the machine. Use a potholder as the handle will be very hot. Let rest for a few minutes.
6. Remove the bread from the pan and allow to cool on a wire rack for at least 10 minutes before slicing.

Nutrition:

- Info (Per Serving):Calories 246, fat 6.7 g, carbs 37.6 g, sodium 146 mg, protein 5.2 g

Blueberry Honey Bread

Servings: 1 Loaf
Cooking Time: 10 Minutes

Ingredients:

- 16 slice bread (2 pounds)
- 1 cup plain yogurt
- ⅔ cup lukewarm water
- ¼ cup honey
- 4 teaspoons unsalted butter, melted
- 2 teaspoons table salt
- 1½ teaspoons lime zest
- ⅔ teaspoon lemon extract
- 4 cups white bread flour
- 2¼ teaspoons bread machine yeast
- 1⅓ cups dried blueberries

Directions:

1. Preparing the Ingredients.
2. Choose the size of loaf of your preference and then measure the ingredients.
3. Add all of the ingredients mentioned previously in the list, except for the blueberries. Close the lid after placing the pan in the bread machine.
4. Select the Bake cycle
5. Turn on the bread machine. White/Basic or Fruit/Nut (if your machine has this setting) setting, select the loaf size, and the crust color. Press start.
6. When the machine signals to add ingredients, add the blueberries.
7. When the cycle is finished, carefully remove the pan from the bread maker and let it rest.
8. Remove the bread from the pan, put in a wire rack to cool for at least 10 minutes, and slice.

Strawberry Shortcake Bread

Servings: 1 Loaf
Cooking Time: 10 Minutes

Ingredients:

- 12 slice bread (1½ pounds)
- 1⅛ cups milk, at 80°F to 90°F
- 3 tablespoons melted butter, cooled
- 3 tablespoons sugar
- 1½ teaspoons salt
- ¾ cup sliced fresh strawberries
- 1 cup quick oats
- 2¼ cups white bread flour
- 1½ teaspoons bread machine or instant yeast

Directions:

1. Preparing the Ingredients.
2. Choose the size of loaf of your preference and then measure the ingredients.
3. Add all of the ingredients mentioned previously in the list. Close the lid after placing the pan in the bread machine.
4. Select the Bake cycle
5. Turn on the bread machine. Select the White/Basic setting, select the loaf size, and the crust color. Press start.
6. When the cycle is finished, carefully remove the pan from the bread maker and let it rest.
7. Remove the bread from the pan, put in a wire rack to cool for at least 2 hours, and slice.

SPICE, NUT & HERB BREAD

Fragrant Herb Bread

Servings: 1 Loaf
Cooking Time: 10 Minutes

Ingredients:
- 12 slices bread (1½ pounds)
- 1⅛ cups water, at 80°F to 90°F
- 1½ tablespoons melted butter, cooled
- 1½ tablespoons sugar
- 1 teaspoon salt
- 3 tablespoons skim milk powder
- 1 teaspoon dried thyme
- 1 teaspoon dried chives
- 1 teaspoon dried oregano
- 3 cups white bread flour
- 1¼ teaspoons bread machine or instant yeast

Directions:
1. Preparing the Ingredients.
2. Choose the size of loaf of your preference and then measure the ingredients.
3. Add all of the ingredients mentioned previously in the list. Close the lid after placing the pan in the bread machine.
4. Select the Bake cycle
5. Turn on the bread machine. Select the White/Basic setting, select the loaf size, and the crust color. Press start.
6. When the cycle is finished, carefully remove the pan from the bread maker and let it rest.
7. Remove the bread from the pan, put in a wire rack to Cool about 10 minutes. Slice

Raisin Seed Bread

Servings: 1 Loaf
Cooking Time: 10 Minutes

Ingredients:

- 12 slice bread (1½ pounds)
- 1 cup plus 2 tablespoons milk, at 80°F to 90°F
- 1½ tablespoons melted butter, cooled
- 1½ tablespoons honey
- ¾ teaspoon salt
- 3 tablespoons flaxseed
- 3 tablespoons sesame seeds
- 1¼ cups whole-wheat flour
- 1¾ cups white bread flour
- 1¾ teaspoons bread machine or instant yeast
- ⅓ cup raisins
-

Directions:

1. Preparing the Ingredients.
2. Choose the size of loaf of your preference and then measure the ingredients.
3. Add all of the ingredients mentioned previously in the list except the raisins.
4. Close the lid after placing the pan in the bread machine.
5. Select the Bake cycle
6. Program the machine for Basic/White bread, select light or medium crust, and press Start.
7. Add the raisins when the bread machine signals, or place the raisins in the raisin/nut hopper and let the machine add them.
8. When the cycle is finished, carefully remove the pan from the bread maker and let it rest.
9. Remove the bread from the pan, put in a wire rack to Cool about 5 minutes. Slice

Olive Bread

Servings:14 Slices
Cooking Time: 3 H.

Ingredients:

- ½ cup brine from olive jar
- Add warm water (110°F) To make 1½ cup when combined with brine
- 2 Tbsp olive oil
- 3 cups bread flour
- 1⅔ cups whole wheat flour
- 1½ tsp salt
- 2 Tbsp sugar
- 1½ tsp dried leaf basil
- 2 tsp active dry yeast
- ⅔ cup finely chopped Kalamata olives

Directions:

1. Add each ingredient except the olives to the bread machine in the order and at the temperature recommended by your bread machine manufacturer.
2. Close the lid, select the wheat, medium crust setting on your bread machine and press start.
3. Add the olives 10 minutes before the last kneading cycle ends.
4. When the bread machine has finished baking, remove the bread and put it on a cooling rack.

Chia Seed Bread

Servings: 14 Slices

Cooking Time: 10 Minutes

Ingredients:

- ¼ cup chia seeds
- ¾ cup hot water
- 2⅜ cups water
- ¼ cup oil
- ½ lemon, zest and juice
- 1¾ cups white flour
- 1¾ cups whole wheat flour
- 2 tsp baking powder
- 1 tsp salt
- 1 Tbsp sugar
- 2½ tsp quick rise yeast

Directions:

1. Preparing the Ingredients
2. Add the chia seeds to a bowl, cover with hot water, mix well and let them stand until they are soaked and gelatinous, and don't feel warm to touch.
3. Add each ingredient to the bread machine in the order and at the temperature recommended by your bread machine manufacturer.
4. Select the Bake cycle
5. Close the lid, select the basic bread, medium crust setting on your bread machine, and press start.
6. When the mixing blade stops moving, open the machine and mix everything by hand with a spatula.
7. When the bread machine has finished baking, remove the bread and put it on a cooling rack.

Pumpkin Coconut Almond Bread

Servings: 12 Slices
Cooking Time: 5 Minutes

Ingredients:

- 1/3 cup vegetable oil
- 3 large eggs
- 1 1/2 cups canned pumpkin puree
- 1 cup sugar
- 1 1/2 teaspoons baking powder
- 1/2 teaspoon baking soda
- 1/4 teaspoon salt
- 1 tablespoon allspice
- 3 cups all-purpose flour
- 1/2 cup coconut flakes, plus a small handful for the topping
- 2/3 cup slivered almonds, plus a tablespoonful for the topping
- Non-stick cooking spray

Directions:

1. Preparing the Ingredients
2. Spray bread maker pan with non-stick cooking spray. Mix oil, eggs, and pumpkin in a large mixing bowl.
3. Mix remaining ingredients together in a separate mixing bowl. Add wet ingredients to bread maker pan, and dry ingredients on top.
4. Select the Bake cycle
5. Select Dough cycle and press Start. Open lid and sprinkle top of bread with reserved coconut and almonds.
6. Set to Rapid for 1 hour 30 minutes and bake. Cool for 10 minutes on a wire rack before serving.

Healthy Basil Whole Wheat Bread

Servings: 10

Cooking Time: 2 Hours

Ingredients:

- Olive oil – 2 tbsps.
- Basil – 1 tbsp.
- Water – 1 1/3 cups
- Whole wheat flour – 4 cups
- Salt – 2 tsps.
- Sugar – 3 tbsps.
- Active dry yeast – 2 tsps.

Directions:

1. Add olive oil and water to the bread pan. Add remaining ingredients except for yeast to the bread pan. Make a small hole into the flour with your finger and add yeast to the hole. Make sure yeast will not be mixed with any liquids. Select whole wheat setting then select light/medium crust and start. Once loaf is done, remove the loaf pan from the machine. Allow it to cool for 5 minutes. Slice and serve.

Grain, Seed And Nut Bread

Servings: 1 Loaf
Cooking Time: 10 Minutes

Ingredients:

- ¼ cup water
- 1 egg
- 3 Tbsp honey
- 1½ tsp butter, softened
- 3¼ cups bread flour
- 1 cup milk
- 1 tsp salt
- ¼ tsp baking soda
- 1 tsp ground cinnamon
- 2½ tsp active dry yeast
- ¾ cup dried cranberries
- ½ cup chopped walnuts
- 1 Tbsp white vinegar
- ½ tsp sugar

Directions:

1. Preparing the Ingredients.
2. Choose the size of loaf of your preference and then measure the ingredients.
3. Add all of the ingredients mentioned previously in the list.
4. Close the lid after placing the pan in the bread machine.
5. Select the Bake cycle
6. Turn on the bread machine. Select the White/Basic setting, select the loaf size, and the crust color. Press start.
7. When the cycle is finished, carefully remove the pan from the bread maker and let it rest.
8. Remove the bread from the pan, put in a wire rack to Cool about 10 minutes. Slice

Simple Garlic Bread

Servings: 1 Loaf
Cooking Time: 10 Minutes

Ingredients:

- 12 slices bread (1½ pounds)
- 1 cup milk, at 70°F to 80°F
- 1½ tablespoons melted butter, cooled
- 1 tablespoon sugar
- 1½ teaspoons salt
- 2 teaspoons garlic powder
- 2 teaspoons chopped fresh parsley
- 3 cups white bread flour
- 1¾ teaspoons bread machine or instant yeast

Directions:

1. Preparing the Ingredients.
2. Choose the size of loaf of your preference and then measure the ingredients.
3. Add all of the ingredients mentioned previously in the list.
4. Close the lid after placing the pan in the bread machine.
5. Select the Bake cycle
6. Turn on the bread machine. Select the White/Basic setting, select the loaf size, and the crust color. Press start.
7. When the cycle is finished, carefully remove the pan from the bread maker and let it rest.
8. Remove the bread from the pan, put in a wire rack to Cool about 10 minutes. Slice

Healthy Spelt Bread

Servings: 10

Cooking Time: 40 Minutes

Ingredients:
- Milk – 1 ¼ cups.
- Sugar – 2 tbsps.
- Olive oil – 2 tbsps.
- Salt – 1 tsp.
- Spelt flour – 4 cups.
- Yeast – 2 ½ tsps.

Directions:
1. Add all ingredients to the bread machine pan according to the bread machine manufacturer instructions. Select basic bread setting then select light/medium crust and start. Once loaf is done remove the loaf pan from the machine. Allow it to cool for 10 minutes. Slice and serve.

Anise Lemon Bread

Servings: 1 Loaf
Cooking Time: 10 Minutes

Ingredients:

- 12 slice bread (1½ pounds)
- ¾ cup water, at 80°F to 90°F
- 1 egg, at room temperature
- ¼ cup butter, melted and cooled
- ¼ cup honey
- ½ teaspoon salt
- 1 teaspoon anise seed
- 1 teaspoon lemon zest
- 3 cups white bread flour
- 2 teaspoons bread machine or instant yeast

Directions:

1. Preparing the Ingredients.
2. Choose the size of loaf of your preference and then measure the ingredients.
3. Add all of the ingredients mentioned previously in the list.
4. Close the lid after placing the pan in the bread machine.
5. Select the Bake cycle
6. Turn on the bread machine. Select the White/Basic setting, select the loaf size, and the crust color. Press start.
7. When the cycle is finished, carefully remove the pan from the bread maker and let it rest.
8. Remove the bread from the pan, put in a wire rack to Cool about 10 minutes. Slice

GLUTEN-FREE BREAD

Sandwich Bread

Servings: 1 Loaf (16 Slices).
Cooking Time: 1 Hour

Ingredients:
- 1 tbsp. active dry yeast
- 2 tbsps. sugar
- 1 cup warm fat-free milk (110° to 115°)
- Two eggs
- 3 tbsps. canola oil
- 1 tsp. cider vinegar
- 2-1/2 cups gluten-free all-purpose baking flour
- 2-1/2 tsp. xanthan gum
- 1 tsp. unflavored gelatin
- 1/2 tsp. salt

Directions:
1. Oil a loaf pan, 9x5 inches in size, and dust with gluten-free flour reserve.
2. In warm milk, melt sugar and yeast in a small bowl—mix yeast mixture, vinegar, oil, and eggs in a stand with a paddle. Slowly whip in salt, gelatin, xanthan gum and flour. Whip for a minute on low speed. Whip for 2 minutes on moderate. The dough will become softer compared to the yeast bread dough that has gluten. Turn onto the prepped pan. Using a wet spatula, smoothen the surface. Put a cover and rise in a warm area for 25 minutes until dough extends to the pan top.
3. Bake for 20 minutes at 375°
4. loosely cover with foil. Bake till golden brown for 10 to 15 minutes more. Take out from pan onto a wire rack to let cool.

Nutrition:
- Info Calories: 110 calories;Total Carbohydrate: 17 g;Cholesterol: 27 mg;Total Fat: 4 g;Fiber: 2 g;Protein: 4 g;Sodium: 95 mg

Gluten-free Whole Grain Bread

Servings: 12

Cooking Time: 3 Hours 40 Minutes

Ingredients:

- 2/3 cup sorghum flour
- 1/2 cup buckwheat flour
- 1/2 cup millet flour
- 3/4 cup potato starch
- 2 1/4 teaspoons xanthan gum
- 1 1/4 teaspoons salt
- 3/4 cup skim milk
- 1/2 cup water
- 1 tablespoon instant yeast
- 5 teaspoons agave nectar, separated
- 1 large egg, lightly beaten
- 4 tablespoons extra virgin olive oil
- 1/2 teaspoon cider vinegar
- 1 tablespoon poppy seeds

Directions:

1. Whisk sorghum, buckwheat, millet, potato starch, xanthan gum, and sea salt in a bowl and set aside.
2. Combine milk and water in a glass measuring cup. Heat to between 110°F and 120°F; add 2 teaspoons of agave nectar and yeast and stir to combine. Cover and set aside for a few minutes.
3. Combine the egg, olive oil, remaining agave, and vinegar in another mixing bowl; add yeast and milk mixture. Pour wet ingredients into the bottom of your bread maker.
4. Top with dry ingredients.
5. Select Gluten-Free cycle, light color crust, and press Start.
6. After second kneading cycle sprinkle with poppy seeds.
7. Remove pan from bread machine. Leave the loaf in the pan for about 5 minutes before cooling on a rack.
8. Enjoy!

Nutrition:

- Info Calories: 153, Sodium: 346 mg, Dietary Fiber: 4.1 g, Fat: 5.9 g, Carbs: 24.5 g, Protein: 3.3 g.

Paleo Bread

Servings: 16
Cooking Time: 3 Hours 15 Minutes

Ingredients:

- 4 tablespoons chia seeds
- 1 tablespoon flax meal
- 3/4 cup, plus 1 tablespoon water
- 1/4 cup coconut oil
- 3 eggs, room temperature
- 1/2 cup almond milk
- 1 tablespoon honey
- 2 cups almond flour
- 1 1/4 cups tapioca flour
- 1/3 cup coconut flour
- 1 teaspoon salt
- 1/4 cup flax meal
- 2 teaspoons cream of tartar
- 1 teaspoon baking soda
- 2 teaspoons active dry yeast

Directions:

1. Combine the chia seeds and tablespoon of flax meal in a mixing bowl; stir in the water and set aside.
2. Melt the coconut oil in a microwave-safe dish, and let it cool down to lukewarm.
3. Whisk in the eggs, almond milk and honey.
4. Whisk in the chia seeds and flax meal gel and pour it into the bread maker pan.
5. Stir the almond flour, tapioca flour, coconut flour, salt and 1/4 cup of flax meal together.
6. Mix the cream of tartar and baking soda in a separate bowl and combine it with the other dry ingredients.
7. Pour the dry ingredients into the bread machine.
8. Make a little well on top and add the yeast.
9. Start the machine on the Wheat cycle, light or medium crust color, and press Start.
10. Remove to cool completely before slicing to serve.

Nutrition:

- Info Calories: 190, Sodium: 243 mg, Dietary Fiber: 5.2 g, Fat: 10.3 g, Carbs: 20.4 g, Protein: 4.5 g.

Cheese & Herb Bread

Servings: 1 Loaf (12 Slices)
Cooking Time: 1 Hour

Ingredients:

- 300ml (1 ¼ cups) warm water
- 60ml (¼ cup) olive oil
- Two egg whites
- One tablespoon apple cider vinegar
- ½ teaspoon baking powder
- 7g (2 teaspoons) dry active yeast
- Two tablespoons granulated sugar
- 200g (2 cups) gluten-free almond flour / or any other gluten-free flour, levelled
- 100g (1 cup) Tapioca/potato starch, levelled
- Two teaspoons Xanthan Gum
- One teaspoon salt
- Two tablespoons grated Parmesan cheese
- One teaspoon dried marjoram
- ¾ teaspoon dried basil
- ¾ teaspoon dried oregano

Directions:

1. According to your bread machine manufacturer, place all the ingredients into the bread machine's greased pan, and select a basic cycle / standard cycle/bake / quick bread / white bread setting. Then choose crust colour, either medium or light, and press start to bake bread.
2. In the last kneading cycle, check the dough
3. it should be wet but thick, not like traditional bread dough. If the dough is too wet, put more flour, one tablespoon at a time, or until dough slightly firm.
4. When the cycle is finished and the machine turns off, remove baked bread from pan and cool on wire rack.

Nutrition:

- Info Calories: 150 Calories;Total fat: 3 g;Cholesterol: 5 mg;Sodium: 415 mg;Carbohydrates: 9 g;Fibre: 1 g;Protein: 4 g

Gluten-free Oat & Honey Bread

Servings: 12
Cooking Time: 3 Hours

Ingredients:

- 1 1/4 cups warm water
- 3 tablespoons honey
- 2 eggs
- 3 tablespoons butter, melted
- 1 1/4 cups gluten-free oats
- 1 1/4 cups brown rice flour
- 1/2 cup potato starch
- 2 teaspoons xanthan gum
- 1 1/2 teaspoons sugar
- 3/4 teaspoon salt
- 1 1/2 tablespoons active dry yeast

Directions:

1. Add ingredients in the order listed above, except for yeast.
2. Make a well in the center of the dry ingredients and add the yeast.
3. Select Gluten-Free cycle, light crust color, and press Start.
4. Remove bread and allow the bread to cool on its side on a cooling rack for 20 minutes before slicing to serve.

Nutrition:

- Info Calories: 151, Sodium: 265 mg, Dietary Fiber: 4.3 g, Fat: 4.5 g, Carbs: 27.2 g, Protein: 3.5 g.

Easy Gluten-free, Dairy-free Bread

Servings: 12

Cooking Time: 2 Hours 10 Minutes

Ingredients:

- 1 1/2 cups warm water
- 2 teaspoons active dry yeast
- 2 teaspoons sugar
- 2 eggs, room temperature
- 1 egg white, room temperature
- 1 1/2 tablespoons apple cider vinegar
- 4 1/2 tablespoons olive oil
- 3 1/3 cups multi-purpose gluten-free flour

Directions:

1. Add the yeast and sugar to the warm water and stir to mix in a large mixing bowl; set aside until foamy, about 8 to 10 minutes.
2. Whisk the 2 eggs and 1 egg white together in a separate mixing bowl and add to baking pan of bread maker.
3. Add apple cider vinegar and oil to baking pan.
4. Add foamy yeast/water mixture to baking pan.
5. Add the multi-purpose gluten-free flour on top.
6. Set for Gluten-Free bread setting and Start.
7. Remove and invert pan onto a cooling rack to remove the bread from the baking pan. Allow to cool completely before slicing to serve.

Nutrition:

- Info Calories: 241, Sodium: 164 mg, Dietary Fiber: 5.6 g, Fat: 6.8 g, Carbs: 41 g, Protein: 4.5 g.

Gluten-free Brown Bread

Servings: 12
Cooking Time: 3 Hours

Ingredients:

- 2 large eggs, lightly beaten
- 1 3/4 cups warm water
- 3 tablespoons canola oil
- 1 cup brown rice flour
- 3/4 cup oat flour
- 1/4 cup tapioca starch
- 1 1/4 cups potato starch
- 1 1/2 teaspoons salt
- 2 tablespoons brown sugar
- 2 tablespoons gluten-free flaxseed meal
- 1/2 cup nonfat dry milk powder
- 2 1/2 teaspoons xanthan gum
- 3 tablespoons psyllium, whole husks
- 2 1/2 teaspoons gluten-free yeast for bread machines

Directions:

1. Add the eggs, water and canola oil to the bread maker pan and stir until combined.
2. Whisk all of the dry ingredients except the yeast together in a large mixing bowl.
3. Add the dry ingredients on top of the wet ingredients.
4. Make a well in the center of the dry ingredients and add the yeast.
5. Set Gluten-Free cycle, medium crust color, and press Start.
6. When the bread is done, lay the pan on its side to cool before slicing to serve.

Nutrition:

- Info Calories: 201, Sodium: 390 mg, Dietary Fiber: 10.6 g, Fat: 5.7 g, Carbs: 35.5 g, Protein: 5.1 g

Italian Parmesan Cheese Bread

Servings: 6 Pcs.
Cooking Time: 1 Hour

Ingredients:

- 300ml (1 ¼ cups) warm water
- 60ml (¼ cup) olive oil
- Two egg whites
- One tablespoon apple cider vinegar
- ½ teaspoon baking powder
- 7g (2 teaspoons) dry active yeast
- Two tablespoons granulated sugar
- 200g (2 cups) gluten-free almond flour / or any other gluten-free flour, levelled
- 100g (1 cup) Tapioca/potato starch, levelled
- Two teaspoons Xanthan Gum
- 28g (¼ cup) grated Parmesan cheese
- One teaspoon salt
- One teaspoon Italian seasoning
- One teaspoon garlic powder

Directions:

1. According to your bread machine manufacturer, place all the ingredients into the bread machine's greased pan and select a basic cycle / standard cycle/bake / quick bread / white bread setting. Then choose crust colour, either medium or light and press start to bake bread.
2. In the last kneading cycle, check the dough
3. it should be wet but thick, not like traditional bread dough. If the dough is too wet, put more flour, one tablespoon at a time, or until dough slightly firm.
4. When the cycle is finished and the machine turns off, remove baked bread from pan and cool on wire rack.

Nutrition:

- Info Calories: 90 Calories;Total fat: 2 g;Cholesterol: 2 mg;Sodium: 48 mg;Carbohydrates: 15g;Fibre: 1 g;Protein: 2 g

Gluten-free Pull-apart Rolls

Servings: 9

Cooking Time: 2 Hours

Ingredients:

- 1 cup warm water
- 2 tablespoons butter, unsalted
- 1 egg, room temperature
- 1 teaspoon apple cider vinegar
- 2 3/4 cups gluten-free almond-blend flour
- 1 1/2 teaspoons xanthan gum
- 1/4 cup sugar
- 1 teaspoon salt
- 2 teaspoons active dry yeast

Directions:

1. Add wet ingredients to the bread maker pan.
2. Mix dry ingredients except for yeast, and put in pan.
3. Make a well in the center of the dry ingredients and add the yeast.
4. Select Dough cycle and press Start.
5. Spray an 8-inch round cake pan with non-stick cooking spray.
6. When Dough cycle is complete, roll dough out into 9 balls, place in cake pan, and baste each with warm water.
7. Cover with a towel and let rise in a warm place for 1 hour.
8. Preheat oven to 400°F.
9. Bake for 26 to 28 minutes; until golden brown.
10. Brush with butter and serve.

Nutrition:

- Info Calories: 568, Sodium: 380 mg, Dietary Fiber: 5.5 g, Fat: 10.5 g, Carbs: 116.3 g, Protein: 8.6 g.

Flax And Sunflower Seeds Bread

Servings: 8 Pcs

Cooking Time: 1 Hour

Ingredients:

- 300ml (1 ¼ cups) warm water
- 60ml (¼ cup) olive oil
- Two egg whites
- One tablespoon apple cider vinegar
- ½ teaspoon baking powder
- 7g (2 teaspoons) dry active yeast
- Two tablespoons granulated sugar
- 200g (2 cups) gluten-free almond flour / or any other gluten-free flour, levelled
- 100g (1 cup) Tapioca/potato starch, levelled
- Two teaspoons Xanthan Gum
- One teaspoon salt
- 55g (½ cup) flax seeds
- 55g (½ cup) sunflower seeds

Directions:

1. According to your bread machine manufacturer, place all the ingredients into the bread machine's greased pan except sunflower seeds.
2. Select basic cycle / standard cycle/bake / quick bread / white bread setting
3. then select crust colour either medium or light and press start.
4. In the last kneading cycle, check the dough
5. it should be wet but thick, not like traditional bread dough. If the dough is too wet, put more flour, one tablespoon at a time, or until dough slightly firm.
6. Add sunflower seeds 5 minutes before the kneading cycle ends.
7. When the cycle is finished and the machine turns off, remove baked bread from pan and cool on wire rack.

Nutrition:

- Info Calories: 90 Calories;Total fat: 2g;Cholesterol: 5 mg;Sodium: 180 mg;Carbohydrates: 18 g;Fibre: 2 g;Protein: 4 g

BASIC BREAD

Black Forest Loaf

Servings: 1 Loaf
Cooking Time: 3 Hours

Ingredients:
- 1 ½ cups bread flour
- 1 cup whole wheat flour
- 1 cup rye flour
- Three tablespoons cocoa
- One tablespoon caraway seeds
- Two teaspoons yeast
- 1 ½ teaspoons salt
- One ¼ cups water
- 1/3 cup molasses
- 1 ½ tablespoon canola oil

Directions:
1. Combine the ingredients in the bread pan by putting the wet ingredients first, followed by the dry ones.
2. Press the "Normal" or "Basic" mode and light the bread machine's crust colour setting.
3. After the cycles are completed, take out the bread from the machine.
4. Cooldown and then slice the bread.

Nutrition:
- Info Calories: 136;Carbohydrates: 27g;Fat: 2g;Protein: 3g

Classic White Bread I

Servings: 1 Loaf
Cooking Time: 10 Minutes

Ingredients:

- 16 slice bread (2 pounds)
- 1½ cups lukewarm water
- 1 tablespoon + 1 teaspoon olive oil
- 1½ teaspoons sugar
- 1 teaspoon table salt
- ¼ teaspoon baking soda
- 2½ cups all-purpose flour
- 1 cup white bread flour
- 2½ teaspoons bread machine yeast

Directions:

1. Preparing the Ingredients
2. Choose the size of bread to prepare. Measure and add the ingredients to the pan in the order as indicated in the ingredient listing. Place the pan in the bread machine and close the lid.
3. Select the Bake cycle
4. Close the lid, Turn on the bread maker. Select the White / Basic setting, then select the dough size and crust color. Press start to start the cycle.
5. When this is done, and the bread is baked, remove the pan from the machine. Let stand a few minutes.
6. Remove the bread from the pan and leave it on a wire rack to cool for at least 10 minutes.
7. After this time, proceed to cut it

Golden Corn Bread

Servings: 1 Loaf
Cooking Time: 10 Minutes

Ingredients:

- 12 to 16 slices bread (1½ to 2 pounds)
- 1 cup buttermilk, at 80°F to 90°F
- ¼ cup melted butter, cooled
- 2 eggs, at room temperature
- 1⅓ cups all-purpose flour
- 1 cup cornmeal
- ¼ cup sugar
- 2¼ cups whole-wheat bread flour
- 1½ teaspoons bread machine yeast

Directions:

1. Preparing the Ingredients.
2. Place the buttermilk, butter, and eggs in your in your bread machine as recommended by the manufacturer.
3. Select the Bake cycle
4. Program the machine for Quick/Rapid bread and press Start. While the wet ingredients are mixing, stir together the flour, cornmeal, sugar, baking powder, and salt in a small bowl.
5. After the first fast mixing is done and the machine signals, add the dry ingredients. When the loaf is done, remove the bucket from the machine. Let the loaf cool for 5 minutes. Gently shake the bucket to remove the loaf, and turn it out onto a rack to cool.

The Easiest Bread Maker Bread

Servings: 12
Cooking Time: 3 Hours

Ingredients:

- 1 cup lukewarm water
- 1/3 cup lukewarm milk
- 3 tablespoons butter, unsalted
- 3 3/4 cups unbleached all-purpose flour
- 3 tablespoons sugar
- 1 1/2 teaspoons salt
- 1 1/2 teaspoons active dry yeast

Directions:

1. Add liquid ingredients to the bread pan.
2. Measure and add dry ingredients (except yeast) to the bread pan.
3. Make a well in the center of the dry ingredients and add the yeast .
4. Snap the baking pan into the bread maker and close the lid.
5. Choose the Basic setting, preferred crust color and press Start.
6. When the loaf is done, remove the pan from the machine. After about 5 minutes, gently shake the pan to loosen the loaf and turn it out onto a rack to cool.
7. Store bread, well-wrapped, on the counter up to 4 days, or freeze for up to 3 months.

Nutrition:

- Info Calories: 183, Sodium: 316 mg, Dietary Fiber: 1.2 g, Fat: 3.3 g, Carbs: 33.3 g, Protein: 4.5 g.

Soft Sandwich Bread

Servings:14 Slices
Cooking Time: 3 H.

Ingredients:

- 2 Tbsp sugar
- 1 cup water
- 1 Tbsp yeast
- ¼ cup vegetable oil
- 3 cups white flour
- 2 tsp salt

Directions:

1. Add each ingredient to the bread machine in the order and at the temperature recommended by your bread machine manufacturer.
2. Close the lid, select the basic bread, low crust setting on your bread machine and press start.
3. When the bread machine has finished baking, remove the bread and put it on a cooling rack.

Onion And Mushroom Bread

Servings: 1 Loaf
Cooking Time: 1 Hour

Ingredients:

- 4 ounces mushrooms, chopped
- 4 cups bread flour
- Three tablespoons sugar
- Four teaspoons fast-acting yeast
- Four teaspoons dried onions, minced
- 1 ½ teaspoons salt
- ½ teaspoon garlic powder
- ¾ cup of water

Directions:

1. Pour the water first into the bread pan, and then add all of the dry ingredients.
2. Press the "Fast" cycle mode of the bread machine.
3. Wait until all cycles are completed.
4. Transfer the bread from the pan into a wire rack.
5. Wait for one hour before slicing the bread into 12 pieces.
6. Servings: 2 ounces per slice

Nutrition:

- Info Calories: 120;Carbohydrates: 25g;Fat: 0g;Protein: 5g

Vegan Cinnamon Raisin Bread

Servings: 1 Loaf
Cooking Time: 3 Hours

Ingredients:

- Two ¼ cups oat flour
- ¾ cup raisins
- ½ cup almond flour
- ¼ cup of coconut sugar
- 2 ½ teaspoons cinnamon
- One teaspoon baking powder
- ½ teaspoon baking soda
- ¼ teaspoon salt
- ¾ cup of water
- ½ cup of soy milk
- ¼ cup maple syrup
- Three tablespoons coconut oil
- One teaspoon vanilla extract

Directions:

1. Put all wet ingredients first into the bread pan, followed by the dry ingredients.
2. Set the bread machine to "Quick" or "Cake" mode.
3. Wait until the mixing and baking cycles are done.
4. Remove the pan from the machine.
5. Wait for another 10 minutes before transferring the bread to a wire rack.
6. After the bread has completely cooled down, slice it and serve.

Nutrition:

- Info Calories: 130;Carbohydrates: 26g;Fat: 2g;Protein: 3g

Whole Wheat Rolls

Servings: 12

Cooking Time: 3 Hours

Ingredients:

- 1 tablespoon sugar
- 1 teaspoon salt
- 2 3/4 cups whole wheat flour
- 2 teaspoons dry active yeast
- 1/4 cup water
- 1 egg
- 7/8 cup milk
- 1/4 cup butter

Directions:

1. All ingredients should be brought to room temperature before baking.
2. Add the wet ingredients to the bread maker pan.
3. Measure and add the dry ingredients (except yeast) to the pan.
4. Make a well in the center of the dry ingredients and add the yeast.
5. Carefully place the yeast in the hole.
6. Select the Dough cycle, then press Start.
7. Divide dough into 12 portions and shape them into balls.
8. Preheat an oven to 350°F. Place rolls on a greased baking pan.
9. Bake for 25 to 30 minutes, until golden brown.
10. Butter and serve warm.

Nutrition:

- Info Calories: 147, Sodium: 236 mg, Dietary Fiber: 3.5 g, Fat: 5.1 g, Carbs: 22.1 g, Protein: 5.1 g.

Vegan White Bread

Servings:14 Slices
Cooking Time: 3 H.

Ingredients:

- 1⅓ cups water
- ⅓ cup plant milk (I use silk soy original)
- 1½ tsp salt
- 2 Tbsp granulated sugar
- 2 Tbsp vegetable oil
- 3½ cups all-purpose flour
- 1¾ tsp bread machine yeast

Directions:

1. Add each ingredient to the bread machine in the order and at the temperature recommended by your bread machine manufacturer.
2. Close the lid, select the basic or white bread, medium crust setting on your bread machine, and press start.
3. When the bread machine has finished baking, remove the bread and put it on a cooling rack.

Homemade Hot Dog And Hamburger Buns

Servings: 8 - 10

Cooking Time: 1 Hour 35 Minutes

Ingredients:

- 1 1/4 cups milk, slightly warmed
- 1 egg, beaten
- 2 tablespoons butter, unsalted
- 1/4 cup white sugar
- 3/4 teaspoon salt
- 3 3/4 cups bread flour
- 1 1/4 teaspoons active dry yeast
- Flour, for surface

Directions:

1. Place all ingredients into the pan of the bread maker in the following order, reserving yeast: milk, egg, butter, sugar, salt, flour.
2. Make a well in the center of the dry ingredients and add the yeast.
3. Select Dough cycle. When cycle is complete, turn out onto floured surface.
4. Cut dough in half and roll each half out to a 1" thick circle.
5. Cut each half into 6 (3 1/2") rounds with inverted glass as a cutter. (For hot dog buns, cut lengthwise into 1-inch-thick rolls, and cut a slit along the length of the bun for easier separation later.)
6. Place on a greased baking sheet far apart and brush with melted butter.
7. Cover and let rise until doubled, about one hour; preheat an oven to 350°F.
8. Bake for 9 minutes.
9. Let cool and serve with your favorite meats and toppings!

Nutrition:

- Info Calories: 233, Sodium: 212 mg, Dietary Fiber: 1.4 g, Fat: 3.8 g, Carbs: 42.5 g, Protein: 6.6 g.

SPECIALTY BREAD

Holiday Eggnog Bread

Servings:1 Loaf
Cooking Time:x

Ingredients:
- 16 slice bread (2 pounds)
- 1½ cups eggnog, at room temperature
- 1½ tablespoons unsalted butter, melted
- 2 tablespoons sugar
- 1¼ teaspoons table salt
- ½ teaspoon ground cinnamon
- ½ teaspoon ground nutmeg
- 4 cups white bread flour
- 1¾ teaspoons bread machine yeast
- 12 slice bread (1½ pounds)
- 1⅛ cups eggnog, at room temperature
- 1⅛ tablespoons unsalted butter, melted
- 1½ tablespoons sugar
- 1 teaspoon table salt
- ⅓ teaspoon ground cinnamon
- ⅓ teaspoon ground nutmeg
- 3 cups white bread flour
- 1⅓ teaspoons bread machine yeast

Directions:

1. Choose the size of loaf you would like to make and measure your ingredients.
2. Add the ingredients to the bread pan in the order listed above.
3. Place the pan in the bread machine and close the lid.
4. Turn on the bread maker. Select the White/Basic setting, then the loaf size, and finally the crust color. Start the cycle.
5. When the cycle is finished and the bread is baked, carefully remove the pan from the machine. Use a potholder as the handle will be very hot. Let rest for a few minutes.
6. Remove the bread from the pan and allow to cool on a wire rack for at least 10 minutes before slicing.

Nutrition:

- Info (Per Serving):Calories 167, fat 2.8 g, carbs 28.6 g, sodium 219 mg, protein 3.8 g

Whole Grain Salt-free Bread

Servings:16

Cooking Time: 3 Hours And 25 Minutes

Ingredients:

- Whole-grain cereal – 2/3 cup
- Water – 1 cup, boiling hot
- Oil – 2 tsp.
- Honey – 4 tsp.
- Orange zest of 1 orange
- Whole wheat flour – 2 cups
- Vital wheat gluten – 4 tsp.
- Active dry yeast – 2 ¼ tsp.

Directions:

1. Add everything in the bread pan in the order listed.
2. Select White/Basic setting. Use the Delay future.
3. Remove the bread when done.
4. Cool, sliced, and serve.

Nutrition:

- Info (Per Serving): Calories: 79; Total Fat: 0.8 g; Saturated Fat: 0.1 g; Carbohydrates: 15.3 g; Cholesterol: 0 mg; Fiber: 0.8 g; Calcium: 5 mg; Sodium: 1 mg; Protein: 2.7 g

Coffee Caraway Seed Bread

Servings:1 Loaf

Cooking Time:x

Ingredients:

- 16 slice bread (2 pounds)
- 1 cup lukewarm water
- ½ cup brewed coffee, lukewarm
- 2 tablespoons balsamic vinegar
- 2 tablespoons olive oil
- 2 tablespoons dark molasses
- 1 tablespoon light brown sugar
- 1 teaspoon table salt
- 2 teaspoons caraway seeds
- ¼ cup unsweetened cocoa powder
- 1 cup dark rye flour
- 2½ cups white bread flour
- 2 teaspoons bread machine yeast
- 12 slice bread (1½ pounds)
- ¾ cup lukewarm water
- ⅓ cup brewed coffee, lukewarm
- 1½ tablespoons balsamic vinegar
- 1½ tablespoons olive oil
- 1½ tablespoons dark molasses
- ¾ tablespoon light brown sugar
- ¾ teaspoon table salt
- 1½ teaspoons caraway seeds
- 3 tablespoons unsweetened cocoa powder
- ¾ cup dark rye flour
- 1¾ cups white bread flour
- 1½ teaspoons bread machine yeast

Directions:

1. Choose the size of loaf you would like to make and measure your ingredients.
2. Add the ingredients to the bread pan in the order listed above.
3. Place the pan in the bread machine and close the lid.
4. Turn on the bread maker. Select the Whole Wheat/Wholegrain setting, then the loaf size, and finally the crust color. Start the cycle.
5. When the cycle is finished and the bread is baked, carefully remove the pan from the machine. Use a potholder as the handle will be very hot. Let rest for a few minutes.
6. Remove the bread from the pan and allow to cool down on a wire rack for at least 10 minutes or more before slicing.

Nutrition:

- Info (Per Serving):Calories 126, fat 1.8 g, carbs 22.6 g, sodium 148 mg, protein 4 g

Challah Bread

Servings:1 Loaf
Cooking Time:x

Ingredients:

- 16 slice bread (2 pounds)
- 1 cup +¾ teaspoon water, lukewarm between 80 and 90^{0}F
- 2 ½ tablespoons unsalted butter, melted
- 2 small eggs, beaten
- 2 ½ tablespoons sugar
- 1 ¾ teaspoons salt
- 4 ½ cups white bread flour
- 2 teaspoons bread machine yeast or rapid rise yeast
- 12 slice bread (1 ½ pounds)
- ¾ cup +1 tablespoon water, lukewarm between 80 and 90^{0}F
- 2 tablespoons unsalted butter, melted
- 1 egg, beaten
- 2 tablespoons sugar
- 1 ½ teaspoons salt
- 3 ¼ cups white bread flour
- 1 ½ teaspoons bread machine yeast or rapid rise yeast
- For oven baking
- 1 egg yolk
- 2 tablespoons cold water
- 1 tablespoon poppy seed (optional)

Directions:

1. Choose the size of loaf you would like to make and measure your ingredients.
2. Add the ingredients to the bread pan in the order listed above.
3. Place the pan in the bread machine and close the lid.
4. Turn on the bread maker. Select the Dough setting, then the loaf size, and finally the crust color. Start the cycle.
5. Lightly flour a working surface and prepare a large baking sheet by greasing it with cooking spray or vegetable oil or line with parchment paper or a silicone mat.
6. Preheat the oven to 375°F and place the oven rack in the middle position.
7. After the dough cycle is done, carefully remove the dough from the pan and place it on the working surface. Divide dough in three even parts.
8. Roll each part into 13-inch-long cables for the 1 ½ pound Challah bread or 17-inch for the 2-pound loaf. Arrange the dough cables side by side and start braiding from its middle part.
9. In order to make a seal, pinch ends and tuck the ends under the braid.
10. Arrange the loaf onto the baking sheet; cover the sheet with a clean kitchen towel. Let rise for 45-60 minutes or more until it doubles in size.
11. In a mixing bowl, mix the egg yolk and cold water to make an egg wash. Gently brush the egg wash over the loaf. Sprinkle top with the poppy seed, if desired.
12. Bake for about 25-30 minutes or until loaf turns golden brown and is fully cooked.

Nutrition:

- Info (Per Serving):Calories 196, fat 3.3g, carbs 33.5 g, sodium 207, protein 6.4g

Cocoa Holiday Bread

Servings:1 Loaf
Cooking Time:x

Ingredients:

- 16 slice bread (2 pounds)
- 1 cup brewed coffee, lukewarm
- ½ cup evaporated milk, lukewarm
- 2 tablespoons unsalted butter, melted
- 3 tablespoons honey
- 1 tablespoon dark molasses
- 1 tablespoon sugar
- 4 teaspoons unsweetened cocoa powder
- 1 teaspoon table salt
- 2¼ cups whole-wheat bread flour
- 2¼ cups white bread flour
- 2¼ teaspoons bread machine yeast
- 12 slice bread (1½ pounds)
- ¾ cup brewed coffee, lukewarm
- ⅓ cup evaporated milk, lukewarm
- 1½ tablespoons unsalted butter, melted
- 2¼ tablespoons honey
- ¾ tablespoon dark molasses
- ¾ tablespoon sugar
- 1 tablespoon unsweetened cocoa powder
- ¾ teaspoon table salt
- 1⅔ cups whole-wheat bread flour
- 1⅔ cups white bread flour
- 1⅔ teaspoons bread machine yeast

Directions:

1. Choose the size of loaf you would like to make and measure your ingredients.
2. Add the ingredients to the bread pan in the order listed above.
3. Place the pan in the bread machine and close the lid.
4. Turn on the bread maker. Select the Sweet setting, then the loaf size, and finally the crust color. Start the cycle.
5. When the cycle is finished and the bread is baked, carefully remove the pan from the machine. Use a potholder as the handle will be very hot. Let rest for a few minutes.
6. Remove the bread from the pan and allow to cool on a wire rack for at least 10 minutes before slicing.

Nutrition:

- Info (Per Serving):Calories 173, fat 2.3 g, carbs 32.4 g, sodium 156 mg, protein 4.4 g

Dry Fruit Cinnamon Bread

Servings:1 Loaf
Cooking Time:x

Ingredients:

- 16 slice bread (2 pounds)
- 1⅔ cups lukewarm milk
- ⅓ cup unsalted butter, melted
- ⅔ teaspoon pure vanilla extract
- ¼ teaspoon pure almond extract
- ⅓ cup light brown sugar
- 1⅓ teaspoons table salt
- 2 teaspoons ground cinnamon
- 4 cups white bread flour
- 1⅔ teaspoons bread machine yeast
- ⅔ cup dried mixed fruit
- ⅔ cup golden raisins, chopped
- 12 slice bread (1½ pounds)
- 1¼ cups lukewarm milk
- ¼ cup unsalted butter, melted
- ½ teaspoon pure vanilla extract
- ¼ teaspoon pure almond extract
- 3 tablespoons light brown sugar
- 1 teaspoon table salt
- 2 teaspoons ground cinnamon
- 3 cups white bread flour
- 1 teaspoon bread machine yeast
- ½ cup dried mixed fruit
- ½ cup golden raisins, chopped

Directions:

1. Choose the size of loaf you would like to make and measure your ingredients.
2. Add all of the ingredients except for the mixed fruit and raisins to the bread pan in the order listed above.
3. Place the pan in the bread machine and close the lid.
4. Turn on the bread maker. Select the White/Basic or Fruit/Nut (if your machine has this setting) setting, then the loaf size, and finally the crust color. Start the cycle.
5. When the machine signals to add ingredients, add the mixed fruit and raisins. (Some machines have a fruit/nut hopper where you can add the mixed fruit and raisins when you start the machine. The machine will automatically add them to the dough during the baking process.)
6. When the cycle is finished and the bread is baked, carefully remove the pan from the machine. Use a potholder as the handle will be very hot. Let rest for a few minutes.
7. Remove the bread from the pan and allow to cool on a wire rack for at least 10 minutes before slicing.

Nutrition:

- Info (Per Serving):Calories 193, fat 4.7 g, carbs 29.3 g, sodium 226 mg, protein 5 g

No-salt White Bread

Servings:12

Cooking Time: 3 Hours And 25 Minutes

Ingredients:

- Warm water - 1 cup
- Olive oil – 1 tbsp.
- Sugar – 1 ¼ tsp.
- Yeast – 1 ¼ tsp.
- Flour – 3 ¼ cup
- Egg white - 1

Directions:

1. Dissolve the sugar in the water.
2. Add yeast to the sugar water.
3. Put flour, yeast mixture, and oil into the bread-maker.
4. Select Basic bread setting.
5. Add the egg white after 5 minutes.
6. Remove the bread when it is done.
7. Cool, slice, and serve.

Nutrition:

- Info (Per Serving): Calories: 275.3; Total Fat: 3 g; Saturated Fat: 0.4 g; Carbohydrates: 52.9 g; Cholesterol: 0 mg; Fiber: 2 g; Calcium: 22 mg; Sodium: 12.2 mg; Protein: 7.9 g

New Year Spiced Bread

Servings:1 Loaf
Cooking Time:x

Ingredients:

- 16 slice bread (2 pounds)
- ½ cup brewed coffee, cooled to room temperature
- ⅔ cup unsalted butter, melted
- ⅔ cup honey
- 1 cup sugar
- ⅓ cup dark brown sugar
- 2 eggs, at room temperature
- 3 tablespoons whiskey
- ⅓ cup orange juice, at room temperature
- 1⅓ teaspoons pure vanilla extract
- 3 cups all-purpose flour
- ⅔ tablespoon ground cinnamon
- ⅔ teaspoon baking soda
- ⅓ teaspoon ground allspice
- ⅓ teaspoon table salt
- ⅓ teaspoon ground cloves
- ⅔ tablespoon baking powder
- 12 slice bread (1½ pounds)
- ⅓ cup brewed coffee, cooled to room temperature
- ½ cup unsalted butter, melted
- ½ cup honey
- ¾ cup sugar
- ¼ cup dark brown sugar
- 2 eggs, at room temperature
- 2 tablespoons whiskey
- ¼ cup orange juice, at room temperature
- 1 teaspoon pure vanilla extract
- 2 cups all-purpose flour
- ½ tablespoon ground cinnamon
- ½ teaspoon baking soda
- ¼ teaspoon ground allspice
- ¼ teaspoon table salt

- ¼ teaspoon ground cloves
- ½ tablespoon baking powder

Directions:

1. Choose the size of loaf you would like to make and measure your ingredients.
2. Add the ingredients to the bread pan in the order listed above.
3. Place the pan in the bread machine and close the lid.
4. Turn on the bread maker. Select the Quick/Rapid setting, then the loaf size, and finally the crust color. Start the cycle.
5. When the cycle is finished and the bread is baked, carefully remove the pan from the machine. Use a potholder as the handle will be very hot. Let rest for a few minutes.
6. Remove the bread from the pan and allow to cool on a wire rack for at least 10 minutes before slicing.

Nutrition:

- Info (Per Serving):Calories 271, fat 8.7 g, carbs 38.3 g, sodium 168 mg, protein 3.4 g

Low-carb Carrot Bread

Servings: 15

Cooking Time: 3 Hours And 25 Minutes

Ingredients:

- Coconut flour - ½ cup
- Xanthan gum - 1/8 tsp.
- Baking powder - ½ tsp.
- Baking soda - ½ tsp.
- Salt - 1/4 tsp.
- Cinnamon - 2 tsp.
- Ginger - ½ tsp.
- Nutmeg - ¼ tsp.
- Granulated sweetener - 2 tbsp.
- Unsweetened almond milk - 1/3 cup
- Butter - ½ cup, melted
- Vanilla extract - 1 tsp.
- Maple extract - 1 tsp.
- Apple cider vinegar - ½ tsp.
- Eggs – 4
- Shredded carrots – 1 ounce

Directions:

1. Add everything in the order recommended by the machine manufacturer.
2. Select Basic bread and crust color. Press Start.
3. Remove the bread when done.
4. Slice, cool, and serve.

Nutrition:

- Info (Per Serving): Calories: 132; Total Fat: 9.4 g; Saturated Fat: 5.9 g; Carbohydrates: 8.8 g; Cholesterol: 60 mg; Fiber: 5.9 g; Calcium: 27 mg; Sodium: 198 mg; Protein: 4.1 g

Holiday Chocolate Bread

Servings:1 Loaf
Cooking Time:x

Ingredients:

- 16 slice bread (2 pounds)
- 1 cup + 3 tablespoons lukewarm milk
- 1 egg, at room temperature
- 2 tablespoons unsalted butter, melted
- 1½ teaspoons pure vanilla extract
- 2⅔ tablespoons sugar
- 1 teaspoon table salt
- 4 cups white bread flour
- 1⅓ teaspoons bread machine yeast
- ⅔ cup white chocolate chips
- ½ cup dried cranberries
- 12 slice bread (1½ pounds)
- ⅞ cup lukewarm milk
- 1 egg, at room temperature
- 1½ tablespoons unsalted butter, melted
- 1 teaspoon pure vanilla extract
- 2 tablespoons sugar
- ¾ teaspoon table salt
- 3 cups white bread flour
- 1 teaspoon bread machine yeast
- ½ cup white chocolate chips
- ⅓ cup dried cranberries

Directions:

1. Choose the size of loaf you would like to make and measure your ingredients.

2. Add all of the ingredients except for the chocolate chips and cranberries to the bread pan in the order listed above.

3. Place the pan in the bread machine and close the lid.

4. Turn on the bread maker. Select the White/Basic or Fruit/Nut (if your machine has this setting) setting, then the loaf size, and finally the crust color. Start the cycle.

5. When the machine signals to add ingredients, add the chocolate chips and cranberries. (Some machines have a fruit/nut hopper where you can add the chocolate chips and cranberries when you start the machine. The machine will automatically add them to the dough during the baking process.)

6. When the cycle is finished and the bread is baked, carefully remove the pan from the machine. Use a potholder as the handle will be very hot. Let rest for a few minutes.

7. Remove the bread from the pan and allow to cool on a wire rack for at least 10 minutes before slicing.

Nutrition:

- Info (Per Serving):Calories 204, fat 4.6 g, carbs 31.7 g, sodium 164 mg, protein 4.5 g

RECIPES INDEX

A

Anise Lemon Bread 71

B

Banana Whole-wheat Bread 55

Basic Honey Bread 40

Basic Sourdough Bread 45

Black Forest Loaf 82

Black Olive Bread 52

Blue Cheese Bread 13

Blueberry Honey Bread 60

Bread Machine Bread 10

Buttermilk Pecan Bread 21

C

Challah Bread 97

Cheese & Herb Bread 75

Cheese Potato Bread 43

Cheesy Sausage Loaf 15

Chia Seed Bread 65

Choco Chip Pumpkin Bread 28

Chocolate Coffee Bread 14

Chocolate Oatmeal Banana Bread 24

Cinnamon Apple Bread 50

Cinnamon Pumpkin Bread 58

Classic Dark Bread 8

Classic White Bread 44

Classic White Bread I 83

Cocoa Holiday Bread 99

Coffee Caraway Seed Bread 95

Craft Beer And Cheese Bread 9

Cranberry Walnut Bread 16

Curd Onion Bread With Sesame Seeds 53

D

Dry Fruit Cinnamon Bread 101

E

Easy Donuts 23

Easy Gluten-free, Dairy-free Bread 77

European Black Bread 39

F

Flax And Sunflower Seeds Bread 81

Fragrant Herb Bread 62

G

German Pumpernickel Bread 36

Gluten-free Best-ever Banana Bread 56

Gluten-free Brown Bread 78

Gluten-free Oat & Honey Bread 76

Gluten-free Pull-apart Rolls 80

Gluten-free Whole Grain Bread 73

Golden Corn Bread 84

Grain, Seed And Nut Bread 68

H

Healthy Basil Whole Wheat Bread 67

Healthy Spelt Bread 70

Herb Sourdough 42

Holiday Chocolate Bread 107

Holiday Eggnog Bread 92

Homemade Hot Dog And Hamburger Buns 91

I

Italian Bread 35

Italian Cheese Bread 22

Italian Parmesan Cheese Bread 79

J
Jalapeno Cheddar Bread 18
Jalapeno Cheese Bread 26
Jalapeño Corn Bread 20
Julekake 7

K
Keto Pumpkin Bread 34

L
Lemon Blueberry Quick Bread 17
Low-carb Apple Bread 38
Low-carb Carrot Bread 106

M
Multigrain Sourdough Bread 41

N
New Year Spiced Bread 104
No-salt White Bread 103

O
Olive Bread 64
Onion And Mushroom Bread 87

P
Paleo And Dairy-free Bread 37
Paleo Bread 74
Paleo Coconut Bread 33
Pecan Apple Spice Bread 47
Pecan Cranberry Bread 46

Portuguese Corn Bread 31
Pumpernickel Bread 11
Pumpkin Coconut Almond Bread 66

R
Raisin Seed Bread 63
Robust Date Bread 54

S
Sandwich Bread 72
Simple Cottage Cheese Bread 25
Simple Garlic Bread 69
Soft Sandwich Bread 86
Sourdough 29
Sourdough Cheddar Bread 49
Sourdough Milk Bread 48
Spicy Cheese Bread 27
Strawberry Shortcake Bread 61
Sweet Challa 32

T
The Easiest Bread Maker Bread 85
Tomato Herb Bread 57

V
Vegan Cinnamon Raisin Bread 88
Vegan White Bread 90

W
Whole Grain Salt-free Bread 94
Whole Wheat Rolls 89

Printed in Great Britain
by Amazon

85180594R00063